'I am delighted to recommend this ~~book~~ on ~~the art of~~ mindful communication. If there is one thing to ~~see in~~ times of great disruption it is that the key to resilient relationships and societies lies in our capacity for authentic dialogue. This is an essential need that all human beings share ... to be recognised, valued and affirmed in our fundamental goodness. Yet, in this age of disembodied social media, while chats go on all the time, we are often left feeling more isolated and discouraged. Thank goodness there is a rise of interest in mindfulness, compassion and now these specific instructions about how to open our hearts and minds with each other in genuine communication. Thank you Frits, Jetty and Victoria and to all the authors! I am confident that this book will benefit countless people.'

Susan Gillis Chapman is a retired Family Therapist, Dharma-teacher, author of *The five keys to mindful communication* (2012) and founder of Green Zone Communication.

'It is wonderful that Frits Koster, Jetty Heynekamp and Victoria Norton have edited this excellent and very timely book on the art of mindful communication. In our digital, disembodied and stressful world, where it's hard to know whom to trust and to find the time for deeper and more meaningful communication, this book has been sorely needed. Now at last we have a practical guide on how to take things deeper and further with one another. With so many people already familiar with mindfulness practices, at least in principle, this invaluable guide can help us all to take some next important steps on the journey.'

Michael Chaskalson, MA, author of *Mindfulness in eight weeks* (2014) and co-author (with Dr. Megan Reitz) of *Mind time* (2018). Professor of Practice adjunct at Hult International Business School (Ashridge) and Associate at the Møller Institute, Churchill College in the University of Cambridge.

'This is a treasure trove of wisdom from a diversity of teachers sharing a diversity of approaches, held together by a common aspiration to enable us all to cultivate our skills in communicating mindfully. As a species, we deeply need wise guidance on how we can integrate compassion and care into our social and relational networks. Let's share this book widely and put into practice the wisdom it offers us!'

Rebecca Crane, PhD, Director, Professor, Centre for Mindfulness Research and Practice, Bangor University, UK, author of *Mindfulness-Based Cognitive Therapy* (2017) and editing author (with Karunavira and Gemma Griffith) of *Essential resources for mindfulness teachers* (2021).

'We are born without our consent or choice, created by DNA, with minds that are responsible for the most amazing compassion but also for the most sadistic cruel and terrifying actions. Despite appeals by many of the contemplative traditions that we must understand the nature of our mind and take responsibility for what they do, it has only been in the last few decades that western science and education have started to explore this as a serious possibility. For too long we have been left ignorant of our minds and vulnerable to the suffering of mental health problems, selfish and anti-social behaviour. However, within schools and workplaces and the flourishing of Internet-based self-training, this is beginning to change. It is therefore a delight, a pleasure and excitement to be able to recommend this wonderfully insightful and practical book that lays out some of the key challenges and opportunities for mindful awareness and compassionate action training. Bringing together some of the top international contributors in the mind training world, I for one will be referring to this book for many years to come and I'm sure others will too.'

Paul Gilbert, OBE, Professor, author of *Compassion Focused Therapy* (2010b), co-author (with Choden) of *Mindful compassion* (2015) and co-editor (with Gregoris Simos) of *Compassion Focused Therapy: clinical practice and applications* (2022).

'We all want good relationships at home and at work, but that's often challenging. Relationships are built from interactions, and interactions are built from communications. The authors of this ground-breaking book show us many ways to communicate honestly and effectively, even during emotionally intense conflicts. With many examples, they bring together the power of mindfulness, deep listening, compassion and skilful assertiveness. Written with great clarity and depth, this is an excellent guidebook to harmonious, fulfilling and productive relationships.'

Rick Hanson, PhD, Senior Fellow of UC Berkeley's Greater Good Science Center, author of *Resilient: How to grow an unshakable core of calm, strength, and happiness* (2018) and other books on positive neuroplasticity.

'This wonderful book explores the art of human communication and connection, and in doing so, takes us to the heart of what our minds most need for healing, growth and for facing the challenges of daily life.'

Charlie Heriot-Maitland, PhD, DClinPsy, Clinical Psychologist and Director of Balanced Minds, and co-author (with Eleanor Longden) of *Relating to voices using Compassion Focused Therapy* (2022).

'This book teaches us interpersonal meditative skills, based on both ancient techniques and modern science to foster our ability to reconnect to others, which seems crucial in these times of polarisation, me-first and us-against-them attitudes.'

Rogier Hoenders, MD, PhD, psychiatrist, Director of the Center for Integrative Psychiatry, Lentis, Groningen and chair of the Dutch consortium for integrative medicine and health.

'If you want to cultivate wisdom and compassion in your relationships, this book offers an accessible and practical guide to getting started. An inspiring collection of six different approaches to becoming a better listener and a more authentic speaker, I highly recommend this book to anyone who values being truly present with those they care about. In a world riddled with conflict and in our day-to-day challenges of living, our shared humanity depends on our collective ability to connect deeply with each other. This book shows you how, so let it be your next step towards mastering the art of mindful communication.'

Mark Hopfenbeck is a social anthropologist specialising in health and social policy, an assistant professor (and mindfulness teacher) at the Norwegian University of Science and Technology (NTNU), visiting fellow at London South Bank University (LSBU) and an individual partner at the Collaborating Centre for Values-based Practice in Health and Social Care, St Catherine's College, Oxford University. He is the co-editor of *The practical handbook of hearing voices* (with Isla Parker and Joachim Schnackenberg, 2021)*, The practical handbook of eating difficulties* (with James Downs et al., 2022) and *The practical handbook of living well with dementia* (with Isla Parker and Richard Coaten, 2022).

'A quality that defines humanity is our capacity for complex communication. But in today's modern world how we communicate with each other has transformed, and not necessarily for the better. We have almost forgotten what it means to be with, listen and share. In this comprehensive book editors Koster, Heynekamp and Norton present six mindful communication programmes that ground us in these most fundamental human qualities of connection and communication. If you want to improve your communication and how you connect with others, this book is a must-have.'

James Kirby, PhD, Clinical Psychologist, Co-Director of the Compassionate Mind Research Group, School of Psychology, The University of Queensland, Australia. Author of *Choose compassion: Why it matters and how it works* (2022).

'This book lets the diamond of mindful communication shine, from various perspectives. A valuable resource to create better human communication.'

Wibo Koole, Director of Centrum voor Mindfulness, The Netherlands and author of *Mindful leadership* (2014).

'We are a social species – historically our survival depended on being part of a group. We need friendship, good relationships, and love; they are associated with good health. In contrast, loneliness and chronic conflict are toxic and associated with many poor health outcomes. This edited collection of original essays draws on ancient wisdom and modern psychology to provide a fresh, engaging and eminently practical set of ideas and tools. It provides a way to realise a vision of the world in which connection, good communication and, yes love, will enable us to meet the challenges of the next 50 years. This is no surprise given the authors' commitment over many years to developing these ideas through deep professional and personal experience, and first and foremost an embodiment of the ideas they extol. It is a stepwise development for the field, applying what we know about mindfulness to communication.'

Willem Kuyken, Ritblat Professor of Mindfulness and Psychological Science, University of Oxford and co-author (with Christina Feldman) of *Mindfulness: Ancient wisdom meets modern psychology* (2019).

'May this book allow many to see clearly and live with awareness of awakening together.'

Florence Meleo-Meyer, Assistant Professor of the Practice, Program Director, Global Relations and Professional Education, Mindfulness Center, Brown University School of Public Health, USA.

'As social beings, people have a deep need to connect with each other. But communicating can be both healing and harming. This book explores how mindfulness and compassion can contribute to people communicating with each other in a more wholesome way. Inspiring examples are offered, from different perspectives, to apply in daily practice. For everyone who is interacting with human beings – and who isn't – this book is warmly recommended. I think our society needs this more than ever before ...'

Anne Speckens, MD, PhD, Professor of Psychiatry and founder and Director of Radboudumc Centre for Mindfulness in Nijmegen, the Netherlands.

'I particularly enjoyed how accessible the book is, with lots of simple examples and a collection of ideas I had some familiarity with but presented in a fresh way with easy-to-use resources. Imagine how much better the world of corporate work could be if the CEO or human resource manager about to have a difficult conversation used some of these approaches.'

Fionnuala Tennyson, Senior Communication Consultant whose former roles include Director of Communications at Kraft Foods Europe, Coca-Cola Enterprises and Chief of Strategic Communications at the United Nations World Food Programme.

'Through mindful communication, the emotional ripples of presence, understanding, empathy, help and support spread out and are replicated across our communities and societies. We desperately need mindful communication, presence and compassion at this point in our evolution, to rise to the challenges we face. This wonderful book offers a powerful and practical guide to helping each of us develop those deep and essential capacities.'

Michael West, CBE, is a Senior Visiting Fellow at The King's Fund, London and Professor of Organisational Psychology at Lancaster University. His latest books include *The courage of compassion* (with Suzie Baily & Ethan Williams, 2020) and *Compassionate leadership* (2021).

Mindful Communication

Skilful communication and warm connection are needed today more than ever before. This book explores the potential of mindfulness skills, and how they can be applied to communication in a range of settings.

Experienced mindfulness teachers and trainers Frits Koster, Jetty Heynekamp and Victoria Norton provide an outline of the mechanisms underlying mindful communication while a selection of experts presents a concise overview of six communication programs that are becoming well-known in the mindfulness world. They describe the background and structure of each course and offer tasters in the form of short exercises and online audio downloads. Each chapter is followed up by further resources, reading lists and web addresses.

Mindful Communication will be of interest to professionals in mental health, social care, education and to anyone who wishes to listen and speak with more wisdom and compassion.

Frits Koster lived as a Buddhist monk in Asia for six years. He is a qualified MBSR, MBCL and IMP teacher and teaches mindfulness and compassion internationally. He is the co-author of various books (Silkworm Books and Routledge). See www.compassionateliving.info or www.fritskoster.com.

Jetty Heynekamp is a qualified physiotherapist who has been practising insight meditation since 1982. She is a certified mindfulness teacher and leads meditation retreats and communication workshops with her husband Frits Koster. She is the co-author of several books.

Victoria Norton is a certified mindfulness teacher whose professional background is in teaching and communications management.

Mindful Communication

Speaking and Listening with Wisdom
and Compassion

Edited by
Frits Koster, Jetty Heynekamp
and Victoria Norton

LONDON AND NEW YORK

Designed cover image: Getty Images

First published 2023
by Routledge
4 Park Square, Milton Park, Abingdon, Oxon OX14 4RN

and by Routledge
605 Third Avenue, New York, NY 10158

Routledge is an imprint of the Taylor & Francis Group, an informa business

British Library Cataloguing-in-Publication Data
A catalogue record for this book is available from the British Library

ISBN: 978-1-032-20053-8 (hbk)
ISBN: 978-1-032-20052-1 (pbk)
ISBN: 978-1-003-26200-8 (ebk)

DOI: 10.4324/9781003262008

Typeset in Times New Roman
by KnowledgeWorks Global Ltd.

Access the Support Material: https://www.routledge.com/9781032200521

Contents

Foreword

Alison Evans

What a treasure chest of jewels on mindful communication – drawing on the experience and generosity of people who have been deeply exploring and articulating mindful ways of being in relationship with others. Each author offers an accessible portal into the practice of being mindful in our relationships, with a collective wisdom unfolding as you turn the pages of this book.

In our personal mindfulness practice, we are forming a deeper relationship with ourselves, listening to our experience, through what is being communicated through the body, heart and mind. As social creatures, we are in relationship with others, spending much of our lives interacting in some form or other. This might include many areas of life; our intimate relationships, family, social, work, neighbours, community, groups we belong to and so on. Opening our practice to this important dimension can aid us to bring our inner practice and intentions for how we wish to live our life, into fruition. How do we wish to be in our communication with others? How do we wish to give and receive in communications?

I remember clearly, my experience of returning home from my first silent mindfulness retreat. I left the retreat feeling so peaceful and in love with the world, only to be enraged by other drivers on the way home, and then irritated by the tiniest of issues with things that weren't to my liking when I landed home! I got pulled up sharply, seeing the strength of my reactivity. Gosh, how does mindfulness serve me here?

How could mindfulness be woven into all my communication? How might I be mindful in those places where there are so many habits and strong patterns built into complex intimate relationships? How to be with people with views that seem different to mine? How to communicate as a woman – balancing what is sometimes referred to as the Yin and Yang of compassion? As we increasingly move to a digital world of communication, that tends to be speeded up, when we are on the move – reactivity can be high. What ways do we want to communicate in this arena?

As mindfulness-based teachers, we step into mindful communication, as part of the role. We are communicating as we guide practice, in the inquiry through deep listening and invitational questions, and through the multitude of ways we attempt to convey themes. We are called to investigate and explore what we want to convey and how to do this. We play with the words we use, the way we use language, the tone of our voice, our non-verbal communication and the important spaces and pauses between the words. We can inquire further into our way of communicating in the midst of teaching. Where are our places of ease and comfort? How do we meet participants? How do we communicate in ways that are inclusive – welcoming of the diversity of experience and background within the group? Communication is a joy, and it has its glitchy moments – what do we do in those moments?

As a mindfulness-based supervisor, I have an avid interest in mindful communication, as it plays an essential part in the process of mindfulness-based supervision. I find it such a joy when two people come together, joined in an embodied presence and sort of dance with listening, speaking, pausing, feeling the resonance of words and each other's presence. Speaking and listening in this mindful way allows conversation to go deeper than the content. We enter a space together where we don't know what will unfold. And this deep listening with whole body and being takes some practice. We need patience. We need reminders. We need some frameworks to support us to navigate. This book offers us many ways of approaching and practising the steps of this dance of relational communication.

In this foreword, I have been touching on some spheres of life where communicating mindfully could make such a difference. I notice the posing of many questions – a continual inquiry and practice. What a wonderful opportunity to be expanding mindfulness practice beyond the individual. Engaging with others to help us grow, moving into honest and open speech, seeing our blind spots and speaking in ways that are true and kind. This book offers an inspiring and comprehensive summary of many approaches to mindful listening and speaking. As you read, you can feel the aliveness and co-creation in communication. Every chapter provides an insight into creative ways of bringing mindful awareness into the realm of relationship. Each author writes in practical and accessible ways, enabling the reader to experiment in their own life. Clear resources and pointers are given to pursue any of these specific frameworks in more detail.

This book is highly relevant and has a wide appeal for mindfulness practitioners, teachers, supervisors, mentors, as well as anyone else, exploring mindfulness within the relational field. My copy has lots of bookmarks in it, I have a sense it is a book I will revisit often. I highly commend this book and the gems of practice within it.

May it be of benefit to you and those you touch in your life.

Alison Evans, DClinRes, Mindfulness-Based Teacher, Trainer and Supervisor. Supervision Lead with the Mindfulness Network, UK. Mindfulness-Based Trainer with the Centre for Mindfulness Research and Practice at Bangor University, UK (with a specialist interest in Mindfulness-Based Supervision).

Foreword

Ernst Bohlmeijer

This collection of essays about mindful communication is a fantastic initiative. Mindfulness has become so established in recent years that it is impossible to imagine our society without it. Where would we be without the gentle but courageous ability to notice what is going on inside us, to explore it with friendliness and curiosity? It stops us from turning away from our inner experiences on the one hand, whilst not letting them run away with us on the other. As I write this foreword, we are in the midst of the Corona crisis and many of us are stuck indoors. There is so much fear, insecurity, frustration and gloom. People who are trained in mindfulness should be thankful that whilst they are certainly not free of these emotions, they have the skills to handle them. After all, the unhealthy handling of emotions and thoughts is one of the quickest routes to developing and strengthening mental health problems.

Mindfulness is a basic life skill. It can help us develop an attentive, friendly, balanced, compassionate and sensitive mind and lead a happier life. This skill benefits ourselves and others, in times of adversity and in times of prosperity.

Developing mindfulness is not always easy, it requires commitment and perseverance. It almost always starts with first confronting one's own inner unease, and many challenges follow on from that. Mindfulness is not a quick fix. Although it is not always easy to pin down its effects in scientific research, a growing number of studies show that mindfulness can contribute to our health and resilience.

We associate mindfulness and meditation with sitting on a cushion, stool or chair, closing our eyes and opening our hands. This is how we learn to direct our attention in the beginning, but mindfulness does not stop when we open our eyes and get up off the cushion. Our skills are put to the test when we go out into the world and meet others. The proof of the pudding is in the eating as they say. You can learn a language from an audiobook, but you only discover whether you have really mastered it when you are in the country where they speak that language.

This is where communication comes into play. We are social beings through and through, experiencing connectedness from birth until death – and the experience of love and interaction with others is essential for our well-being, something has become very clear to us during the Corona crisis. We thrive in friendly, loving and caring relationships, for example, at home, with family, at work and in various communities. But at the same time relating well to others is our greatest challenge. It is so easy to get hurt, something which is borne out by the struggles we experience in our relationships with others. On the other hand, to what extent are we living disconnectedly alongside each other, not really listening? And just think how much pain could be saved and how relationships could be even more satisfactory if we were able to listen and speak more attentively. That is what this book is all about.

After a general introduction to mindful communication, there are six introductions to different programmes and methods. The most famous is possibly Non-Violent Communication, developed by Marshall Rosenberg, but the other training programmes are also becoming better known. They are all interesting and presented by people who know them in depth. This makes it an ideal introduction, the reader gets a taste of each one, but as the book offers examples and techniques to try out, it will seem like more than just dipping a toe in the water.

I am convinced that the world would look very different if we took the wisdom in this book on board. It encourages us to live from our hearts and to be careful and caring with ourselves and others. Who knows, one day it may just lead to two souls sharing one experience. What more could a human being want?

Ernst Bohlmeijer, Professor of Mental Health Promotion at the University of Twente, the Netherlands and co-author of several self-help books on the art of living, such as A Beginners guide to mindfulness (2013) and Using positive psychology every day (2018).

Acknowledgements

Let us be grateful to the people who make us happy;
they are the charming gardeners who make our souls blossom.
Marcel Proust (1871–1922)

Feeling gratitude and appreciation is very important for well-being (Wong et al., 2016). Many people have contributed to the writing of this book, and we would like to thank them very much. First of all, we are very grateful to our meditation teachers for having introduced us to the world of mindfulness and compassion. To the founders of the programmes discussed in this book, we also offer our sincere thanks and appreciation for all their dedication. We know from experience how much time, space, patience and equanimity it takes to initiate and develop something as valuable as the mindful communication programmes presented here.

We are especially indebted to all the co-authors of this book for their willingness to share their wisdom. They, in turn, have expressed their heartfelt thanks to their co-readers for their efforts and helpful reading of and suggestions for the texts in this book. Thanks also to Alison Evans and Ernst Bohlmeijer for their beautiful and heartfelt forewords. Many thanks also to the following for their kind endorsements: Susan Gillis Chapman, Michael Chaskalson, Rebecca Crane, Paul Gilbert, Rick Hanson, Charlie Heriot-Maitland, Rogier Hoenders, Mark Hopfenbeck, James Kirby, Wibo Koole, Willem Kuyken, Florence Meleo-Meyer, Anne Speckens, Fionnuala Tennyson and Michael West.

Thank you for supporting our intention. We are very grateful to Christian Stocker for his wonderful drawings in Chapter 1.

Many thanks to our Dutch publisher (Boom) and to Joanne Forshaw, Daradi Patar and all their colleagues from Routledge Taylor & Francis Group UK, who have also published our previous two English language books on the Mindfulness-Based Compassionate Living or MBCL compassion training. Thank you for your trust and for supporting our vision of a more compassionate world.

We would also like to express our appreciation to all the participants in the programmes covered in this book. Without their courage and willingness to take part in the communication programmes described in this book, which can sometimes be challenging and bring us into contact with painful areas within ourselves, the programmes would not have come to be.

Thich Nhat Hanh, the Vietnamese meditation teacher, who recently passed away, sometimes said 'No mud, no lotus.' We are immensely grateful for the difficulties we have experienced in our life; they may have functioned as a valuable condition for our interest in developing mindfulness, wisdom and compassion. Last but not least we are very grateful for our friendship and for having been able to work together as an editing team. It really confirmed the beautiful African saying: 'If you want to go fast, go alone. But if you want to go far, go together.'

Frits Koster, Jetty Heynekamp & Victoria Norton,
January 2023

How this book came about

Wise communication is not always easy. To give an example: many communication problems occur at the end of meetings. We feel that we have just a few minutes left to address an important topic or make a quick decision and we become impatient. As a result, our attention decreases which in no time at all can lead to all sorts of lumps and bumps in our communication with others. The social intelligence of the people who experience high levels of happiness, satisfaction and connectedness appears to be higher than their cognitive intelligence. We think the ability to communicate wisely and compassionately could be a major factor in this.

Our own search

Some people are naturally very adept communicators, but for others, it is a bit of a blind spot. This can have many reasons, for example, growing up in a family where there was little genuine communication, or having had a dominant, punitive parent who was not a good role model. In this foreword, we want to share something about our own search and about the intention of this book.

Frits

I (Frits) grew up the middle child of three in a family where there was little real communication. Fortunately, I had a sister with whom I could share a lot; however, because of the many quarrels between my brother and my sister, I learned to adapt well to others and to appease conflicts, but my own needs were not really addressed. I had a very good relationship with my father, but he was quite introverted and didn't talk much, so it wasn't very usual for us to have a heart-to-heart about personal matters or current affairs. I experienced an identity crisis as a young man and in 1979 I came into contact with the practice of meditation and the Buddhist philosophy of life. I was very touched by the practice of vipassana or insight meditation, a practice in which the development of mindfulness or awareness is central. I also felt a deep connection with Buddhist psychology, which was so strong that in 1982 – instead of starting to study psychology – I went to South-East Asia and meditated and studied as a monk for over five years in various monasteries and meditation centres in Thailand, Myanmar and Sri Lanka.

When I returned to the Netherlands in 1988, I gradually began to see a gap in the training I had received in South-East Asia. In Asia, I had become well-versed in the study of Buddhist psychology and in meditation, and I had also become very familiar with ethical guidelines or life advice, which were aimed at avoiding harm to myself and others. But not much attention was paid to how you could communicate with others with more mindfulness, wisdom and compassion. And the more intimate the relationship, the more difficult it turned out to be to communicate wisely. In this way, I gradually developed a deeper need to be able to integrate the valuable quality of mindfulness into everyday life.

Jetty

I (Jetty) come from a family of four children, of whom I am the eldest. My father was a very authoritarian man who did not tolerate any contradiction. As a result, I always kept myself as quiet as I could as a child because that was the safest thing to do. Because of this, we had few in-depth conversations and discussions at home and we didn't talk about much other than daily domestic matters, even when I was a teenager. So my family was not in a position to equip me to talk about emotions and to deal with conflicts or to talk them out.

At the age of 18, I left home to study. I yearned for something deeper and tried all kinds of yoga, including meditation. At the age of 25, I came into contact with vipassana meditation and the concept of awareness and felt that was what I had been looking for. I went to Sri Lanka a couple of times for a six-week retreat, but eventually I decided not to become a nun there because I had some concerns about the position of nuns and women in general in Sri Lanka at that time. I chose to continue my meditation path in the Netherlands. I married and had two children, and in raising the children, my experience with the practice of mindfulness proved to be of great value. I was able to recognise my own patterns so that I did not inadvertently pass them on to the next generation.

The marriage did not work out and in 2003 Frits and I got to know each other. A few years after that, we got married. Even today we still notice how important it is to communicate well with each other.

Victoria

I (Victoria) graduated in the United Kingdom in 1983 during a recession. There were few jobs for graduates so I decided to do a postgraduate certificate in education and taught in a secondary school. It wasn't what I had planned to do and it was very stressful, but I discovered my talent for communicating complex ideas simply and making learning fun. After falling in love and moving to Germany, I retrained for a management position. For many years, I worked for a global company in the communication department dealing mostly with customers and critical stakeholders who were sometimes upset because the company hadn't fulfilled their expectations. I learned how helpful it was to kindly acknowledge their feelings and just listen. So, like many people, communication has been a big part of my professional life. Just reducing reactivity by pausing, taking a step back and really tuning in to the situation can make a world of difference – and hopefully as more people discover mindful communication – bring about a more compassionate and less polarised world.

The intention for writing this book

Research has clearly shown that mindfulness-based programmes can help prevent empathy fatigue and burnout, and contribute to self-awareness, self-compassion and empathic capacity (Karpowicz, Harazduk & Haramati, 2009; Saunders et al., 2007; Shapiro, Astin, Bishop & Cordova, 2005; Shapiro, Brown & Biegel, 2007). According to Professor of Psychiatry and scientist Stephen Porges (2017), mindful and caring communication also appears to have a calming effect. Expressed in a simple and poetic way: sharing is repairing. And the healing effect of listening with open attention was expressed by one participant as follows: 'You have made me visible by listening.'

In this book, we have chosen six communication programmes that can support us in developing the art of wise and compassionate communication, not all of which are well-known. We have focused on secular, non-religious training programmes, in which mindfulness plays an implicit or explicit role. This does not mean that we want to treat the religious backgrounds from which some programmes originated with disrespect. In addition, we are aware that there may also be other very valuable forms of communication training. There is, for example, the Socratic dialogue, which teaches us to ask questions that are both connective and in-depth. There are also very valuable forms of communication that have their origins in the old indigenous American tradition, such as the Council Circle. In *The way of council* (2009) Jack Zimmermann and Virginia Coyle describe how this special intimate form of conversation can be used in all kinds of communities.[1]

On the Internet, you can also find simple memory aids to promote wise speech, such as the THINK acronym. Here THINK stands for a reflection: Is it True? Is it Helpful? Is it Inspiring? Is it Necessary? Is it Kind?

Wisdom and compassion can flourish with the help of a training programme. In this book, we have chosen communication programmes that we know well from the inside out and that are accessible to everyone, regardless of religion, belief or skin colour. This makes implementation in, for example, education and (mental) healthcare more acceptable. We realise that in this book we can only offer a brief description of these enormously rich programmes. However, this introduction does present an opportunity for readers to explore them, thus providing a little taste. We hope that this will inspire further exploration.

For whom is the book intended?

This book is primarily aimed at care workers, such as doctors, psychologists, social workers and nurses. In addition, the book is very suitable for other professionals who work with people, such as coaches, managers, teachers and trainers. But it is also interesting for anyone who deals with other people, which is most of us! The style of the book is non-academic and scientific references are kept to a minimum and reproduced at the back of the book so as not to obstruct the flow of the text. We did not have a clear hierarchical intention in the arrangement of the programmes, and they all have their unique characteristics and perspectives. We are aware that we have by no means been able to cover all existing communication programmes.

For readers who have little or no experience in the practice of mindfulness, we have provided some basic mindfulness exercises as free downloadable and audio exercises on page 125. Here you can also find other audio exercises, which are usually indicated at the end of each chapter in the section 'Resources', ◀⟩). If you still have little experience with the practice of mindfulness and become more interested as a result of one of the programmes in this book, we recommend that you enrol in a mindfulness training course, such as MBSR or MBCT training, Breathworks, Acceptance and Commitment Therapy (ACT), Mindfulness-Based Relapse Prevention (MBRP) or Dialectic Behavioural Therapy (DBT). This is actually a prerequisite for the Interpersonal Mindfulness training described in Chapter 3.

The authors

We are very honoured that these authors were willing to write a chapter for this book. All the authors are experts in the programme they write about and they have a rich experience in the field of mindfulness, secular and/or from a meditative tradition. We are very grateful for their cooperation.

At the time of writing this book, the (effect of the) Corona pandemic is still clearly present in the world, the world is bleeding from intolerance and violence and we are suffering from the vast and rapid changes in the climate. Precisely at a time when we are being so painfully confronted with our human vulnerability, many people have become particularly aware of the importance of the quality of connection, diversity, inclusion and care both for ourselves and with others.

We have therefore agreed that 50% of the proceeds from the sale of the book will automatically be transferred to the Mindfulness Network UK charity as a donation.[2] We hope that this book can help readers to develop greater flexibility and care in speaking and listening with mindfulness, wisdom and compassion.

Frits Koster, Jetty Heynekamp & Victoria Norton,
January 2023

Notes

1 In a Council Circle, participants sit in a circle and use a so-called 'talking stick', which is always picked up or passed on by one of the participants. The one with the talking stick has the intention of really speaking from authenticity, those who listen can practice open and empathetic listening. For more information, see www.waysofcouncil.net.

2 The Mindfulness Network has the intention to reduce/alleviate human suffering, promote well-being and create the conditions in which people, communities and the planet can flourish, by offering activities and services for developing mindfulness and compassion both internally and in society. See www.mindfulness-network.org/ for more information about the Mindfulness Network.

Chapter 1

Introduction

The value of mindful communication

Frits Koster, Jetty Heynekamp and Victoria Norton

> *We have profound differences from other animals, and that is both a blessing and a curse.*
>
> Paul Gilbert[1]

We are in constant dialogue with ourselves and with others. In his description of the spirit or psyche, clinical professor of psychiatry Siegel (2010) expresses this as an 'emergent, self-organizing, embodied, and relational process that regulates the flow of energy and information'. This definition highlights how we as human beings, living with a body and a mind, are constantly engaged in a reciprocal relationship with ourselves and with others. It also shows how we process and react to a flow of energy and information, and from there communicate with ourselves and with others again.

The complex human brain

Thanks to our complex brain, we can communicate in very complex ways. This extraordinary organ has evolved over many millions of years and has helped us to survive. However, it has developed slowly and it is often difficult for the brain to handle modern developments, such as the over-stimulation of our modern life and phenomena such as social media. A model by the American physician and neuroscientist MacLean (1990) can help us understand the structure of our brains. This model distinguishes three layers:

The reptilian brain. This oldest part of our brain is estimated to be five hundred million years old and coordinates all kinds of automatic processes and instinctive reactions. It focuses on fighting, fleeing, freezing, feeding (including digesting) and procreating.

The old mammalian brain, also known as the 'emotional brain'. This gradually emerging part is aimed at living together in agrarian societies with peers and handling rivalry and hierarchical positioning for rank, attachment and care.

DOI: 10.4324/9781003262008-1

The new mammalian brain or neocortex. This newest part of our brain emerged even later in evolution and enables us to imagine and remember things, plan, interpret, reflect, reason, fantasize and express ourselves in language.

This perhaps very simplistic and outdated model serves only to illustrate how complex we are, with a brain that encompasses millions of years of evolution and which can make us react in many ways. This brain offers us unprecedented possibilities, but it does not always function adequately as these three different parts do not always work well together. Sometimes instinctive reactions are the best option, such as when a car suddenly approaches us at high speed. Doing a mindfulness exercise will not help in this situation, only jumping aside as quickly as possible will. But even in situations that are not immediately life-threatening such as a meeting, the reptile brain can dominate the rational brain and cause an inadequate response for example, by making us erupt in anger. The new brain can also exaggerate something that has been said, causing us to ruminate, activate the reptilian brain and become unnecessarily entangled in a stress reaction.

The new brain enables us to come up with the most creative inventions and has helped us to become the most powerful animal species on the earth. But we can also be controlled by destructive reactions which seriously damage our relationships with others. It is not our fault that we were born with an erratic, incalculable brain, but we can consider it a challenge and take on the responsibility of dealing with it as wisely and compassionately as possible.

A ray of hope

Fortunately, we are not entirely at the mercy of the whims of our brains. Daniel Siegel (2007) and others nowadays speak of a *mindful brain*, as a whole new development in our brain. When we learn to contemplate our thoughts, feelings and emotions with mindfulness, we can gradually develop a mindful brain. *Homo Sapiens Sapiens* could then truly be called the human being who knows that they know and can therefore communicate more skilfully with themselves and with others.

Mindfulness

Everyone has moments of mindfulness, but for many this is an underdeveloped ability. The phenomenon 'mindfulness' can be defined in many different ways (Feldman & Kuyken, 2019). One way of defining it, is 'being aware of an experience in an open, non-judgemental way in the present moment'. Mindfulness thus focuses on what is happening in the present and is aware of it, without judging or analysing it.

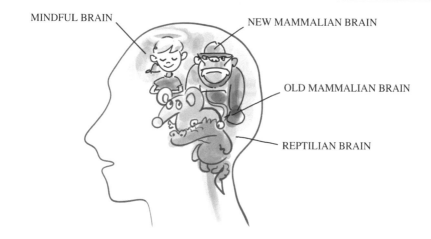

MINDFUL BRAIN   NEW MAMMALIAN BRAIN

OLD MAMMALIAN BRAIN

REPTILIAN BRAIN

Figure 1.1 The evolved brain.

© Christian Stocker

Meditative awareness training has been around for centuries and has an important place in Eastern philosophies. In the West, mindfulness became popular in the 1970s when the American molecular biologist Kabat-Zinn (1990) developed the secular Mindfulness-Based Stress Reduction (MBSR) programme at the hospital of the University of Massachusetts. It was inspired by Eastern awareness practices for patients suffering from chronic pain, physical limitations, otherwise difficult-to-treat conditions and all kinds of stress-related complaints. He defines mindfulness as 'the awareness that arises from being deliberately attentive in the present moment, without having to judge, in the service of developing self-insight and wisdom'. The MBSR training proved to be very helpful in dealing with pain and stress in a novel way.

In the 1990s, Zindel Segal, Mark Williams and John Teasdale (second edition 2013) searched for scientifically based methods to prevent the recurrence of depression. They introduced Mindfulness-Based Cognitive Therapy (MBCT) into mental healthcare, a variation of MBSR with more emphasis on dealing skilfully with rumination, which has proved to be effective in preventing relapse. Both training courses are non-religious in nature and were developed within modern healthcare and gradually the practice of mindfulness has also become more and more common in other fields.

Three motivation systems in communication situations

We included an additional simple, insightful model in a compassion training we developed.[2] The model comes from Gilbert (2010b) and distinguishes three very basic emotion regulation systems: a threat system, a drive system and a soothing system.

Take, for example, a cat. When a cat feels safe and has eaten a good meal, it will lie down in the sun or groom itself or another cat. It is relaxed; the calming system dominates at that moment. However, if it suddenly hears a strange dog bark, then it will jump up, arch its back and start hissing. The attention is suddenly completely focused on the threat, the danger system is activated and the cat is on alert. When the danger has passed, it lies down again.

When it suddenly sees a mouse, it is fully alert and focused again, but the atmosphere is different from when it felt threatened. Now it is after its prey or reward. This is also called the drive system. Once it has caught the mouse and possibly eaten it, the cat goes back to rest.

This model provides a simple understanding of how all animals, including humans, function, and how they are motivated. We need all three systems in order to survive.

The threat system

The threat system is the most fundamental system and is triggered when we feel threatened physically or mentally. Attention is focused on the threat. The emotions we experience are fear, panic, aggression, suspicion and resistance and the corresponding behaviour is fighting or fleeing, freezing or fainting. Trauma specialists distinguish two other biological stress reactions: when fleeing is not possible, we can also react with fawning, submission or dissociation. Finally, according to research by Taylor (2006), we can also react with a tend and befriend reaction; we are then instinctively focused on protecting or making friends with others in order to survive.

The drive system

The drive system is activated when we are driven by longing and desire. It is aimed at satisfying needs for food, sex, success, status, recognition or power. Attention is narrowed, just as with the threat system, but the focus is now on obtaining a reward. The emotions are usually pleasant, but brief. The drive system is all about desire, excitement, kicks, vitality and pleasure. The accompanying behaviour is driven and focused on getting rewards, but it can also lead to addiction and/or exhaustion.

The soothing system

The soothing system is activated when we are not under stress. Attention is open and relaxed. In mammals, the system also focuses on inner and social connection, harmony and well-being. As with the drive system, the emotions are pleasant, but they are long lasting and bring more peace and satisfaction. We experience the peace and tranquillity of the 'being mode', which can also express itself when we *do* something in a relaxed way, such

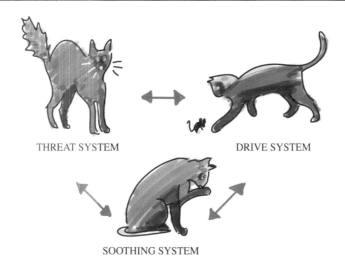

THREAT SYSTEM   DRIVE SYSTEM

SOOTHING SYSTEM

Figure 1.2 Three emotion regulation systems.

© Christian Stocker

as taking a leisurely walk. In the soothing system, it is all about warmth, calmness, well-being, playfulness and solidarity.

Communicating from the soothing system

The model of the three systems provides a simple insight into our human 'hardware' and this can be very helpful when interacting with others. After all, we can often feel which system is in the foreground in the present moment in the body, for example, our physical posture, our way of breathing or the tension or relaxation in specific muscles.

We need all the three systems to survive, but especially the drive and threat systems can influence our communications with others in unhelpful ways. Both approaches cost a lot of energy. The programmes described in this book all show how communicating more from the soothing system is less draining and much more productive because we are not caught up in striving to solve other people's problems which might make the other parties feel threatened, or acting out of our own feelings of threat. As the programmes in this book demonstrate, communication is then less stressful and more productive.

The value of mindfulness for professionals working with people

The value of mindfulness in therapeutic relationships is being increasingly recognised in the scientific literature (Hick & Bien, 2008; Wilson & DuFrene, 2008). It is not always easy to provide care and remain in balance. Many people who work with people experience clear symptoms of burnout at least once in their working life. The National Survey on Working Conditions (NEA) regularly conducts surveys in the UK. In the latest one undertaken in 2021, one in five employees struggled with burnout complaints.[3]

Halifax (2019), a well-known contemporary American meditation teacher, anthropologist and initiator of Upaya, an institute focussed on bringing about social transformation and justice in the world and providing compassionate care for the most vulnerable, describes five so-called 'edge states'. The word 'edge' refers to the edge of a high mountain on which we stand, as it were. We can enjoy the beautiful view, but we have to be careful not to fall. These five edge states or 'tipping points' are altruism, empathy, integrity, respect and engagement. These are qualities common in health and social care and the idea of 'edge states' may explain why people in these professions are so prone to burnout.

Altruism or selflessness can be defined as carrying out selfless actions that promote the welfare of others. There is a clearly healthy side to this, we are lifted above ourselves and become a bright beacon in the world. Our life is expanding from living in an ego system to living in a generous ecosystem. However, there is also a pitfall if we focus too much on altruism, forgetting (and losing sight of) our own needs or even falling into 'pathological altruism', where we feel we have to help others at all costs.

Empathy manifests itself as empathy for pain and suffering. Halifax distinguishes three types of empathy. First of all, we can physically experience empathy in the body as the direct resonance of the confrontation with pain and suffering – she calls this somatic empathy. We can also experience emotional empathy, and finally, we can also experience it cognitively, as we endeavour to understand the circumstances which the other person is experiencing. All three forms of empathy are important. The pitfall of empathy is called empathy distress. This occurs when we ourselves start to suffer from the pain of others. Social workers who feel overwhelmed by their work often use the term 'compassion fatigue'. Ricard (2015) argues that this term is actually incorrect because you don't get exhausted from being compassionate if it includes self-compassion. 'Empathy fatigue' is therefore a more appropriate term.

Integrity or a sense of justice is a sincere commitment to moral and ethical values and standards, and the courage to stand up for these values when necessary. The value of integrity is that it engenders reliability; people of integrity are highly regarded in society. However, we can also suffer from integrity. We can experience moral pain, for example, when we are powerless in the face of injustice. We can experience moral injury if, in a given circumstance, we have been forced to cross ethical boundaries ourselves and are tortured internally by feelings of remorse, guilt and shame. We can be hurt if we cannot find a way out of moral outrage when we have to deal with ethical injustices caused by others. Finally, we can experience moral apathy when we have had to deal with injustice for a long time and have closed ourselves off because we feel powerless.

Respect is the basis for dignity, harmony, humility and wise care. Respect creates space, and it works like the connective tissue in a healthy relationship. It expresses itself in respect for others, for other beliefs, values and norms, and as self-respect. There are several pitfalls to respect. Bullying or harassment, for example, is a sign of a lack of respect. We can not only experience disrespect from classmates or colleagues, but also from people who have a higher or a lower position hierarchically. Finally, we can also have a lack of respect for ourselves, by developing a hard inner critic, or by mercilessly neglecting ourselves.

Engagement manifests itself as a healthy dedication or enthusiasm in relation to our work and in being of service to others. This ensures fulfilment of our life's values and gives us satisfaction. The downside of engagement is excessive involvement, which may lead to workaholism, exhaustion and burnout.

Compassion

Halifax mentions the value of compassion for helping us be more aware of the shadow sides of the qualities mentioned, so they don't pull us over the edge. Compassion can be defined as a sensitive attitude to pain and suffering in ourselves and in others, accompanied by a willingness to make an effort to alleviate or prevent this suffering. Nowadays a distinction is made between 'yin compassion' and 'yang compassion'. In yin compassion, we or others benefit more from a gentle expression of compassion, which can manifest as comfort, gentleness and understanding. At other times, there is a greater need for the courage, steadfastness and constancy of 'yang compassion'.[4]

In healthcare, education, coaching, management and other fields of work where a lot of communication takes place, we meet the five edge states in all sorts of ways. They can be a guideline for a happy and connected life, but we can also stumble into the accompanying pitfalls. It is as if, in communicating with people, we are always walking on a tightrope. Here the practice of mindfulness can be a great support.

Kabat-Zinn regularly gives an alternative definition of mindfulness, describing it as a training in 'relationality'.[5] He explains this as 'how we relate to everything, including our body and mind, our thoughts and emotions, our past and what has shaped us into the present – and how we can be in every aspect of our lives with integrity, with wisdom and with kindness to ourselves and to others'.

Wisdom and compassion

> *Remember that just as a bird needs two wings to fly, wisdom and compassion must be developed simultaneously.*
>
> Ancient saying

This beautiful metaphor shows that mindfulness is not completely without intention. It enables us to cultivate two valuable qualities: wisdom and compassion.

Armstrong (2011), a historian in comparative religious studies, found compassion to be the core value of all major religions. This appears also to be the case with wisdom. According to a description in Buddhist psychology, wisdom or clear comprehension investigates and penetrates the reality of things. It sheds light in the darkness, creates clarity and is the antithesis of misunderstanding, confusion or ignorance.

Glück (2016), professor of Developmental Psychology at the Alpen-Adria University in Klagenfurt, Austria, has been researching wisdom for many years, developing new approaches for defining and measuring wisdom. Wisdom is considered to be a state and not a trait, it can be developed by life experience but this is not necessarily always the case, as is expressed by Oscar Wilde: 'With old age comes wisdom but sometimes old age comes alone'. Glück explores why it is that many people age but not everyone becomes wiser, and describes five principles for a fulfilled or successful life, highlighting the qualities we need to be able to learn from life's inevitable challenges:[6]

- *Openness.* We embody wisdom when we are interested in new ideas and perspectives and are tolerant of people who do not share our views. Wise people do not aim to surround themselves only with like-minded others, as so many of us do in these polarizing times, but to listen respectfully to people with different views and thus broaden their perspective.
- *Emotion regulation.* This principle expresses the willingness to consider one's own and others' emotions as indicators of important aspects of a situation, not just as something that needs to be either suppressed or fully expressed. Wise people are attentive to emotions and take them seriously, but they are skilled at regulating them as a situation requires.
- *Empathy.* This quality implies a sensitivity to others and to ourselves affectively and cognitively.
- *Reflectivity.* This fourth facet of the diamond of wisdom includes a truth-seeking attitude – it's about wanting to understand complex issues in all their complexity, including wanting to understand and know ourselves with all our ambiguities, weaknesses and blind spots. We have the courage to take a new perspective and gain a new insight, even if it complicates things.[7]
- *Recognition of uncontrollability.* Everything in life ultimately turns out to be impermanent and beyond our control. This doesn't mean we should accept everything. We may refer to the words that have become known as the Serenity prayer: 'Grant me the serenity to accept the things I cannot change, the courage to change the things I can, and the wisdom to know the difference'. Understanding and

wise management of uncontrollability that is common to all humanity can paradoxically bring us some inner space that was expressed by John of the Cross as 'Tenderly I touch all things, knowing that one day we shall have to depart'.

Germer and Siegel (2014) have defined wisdom very practically in a contemporary secular context as 'knowing how to live'. They have distinguished eight types of wisdom, which are all in accordance with the five principles as described by Glück:

- Stepping out of the thought stream
- Being with discomfort
- Disengaging from automatic responses
- Transpersonal insight
- Moment-to-moment observation of the mind's antics
- Seeing how the mind creates suffering
- Embracing opposites
- Developing compassion

The emerging science of evidence-based wisdom confirms that wisdom is a very important quality not only for us as individuals but also for meeting the many challenges of the fragile world we live in. In their book *Wisdom: The psychology of wise thoughts, words and deeds,* Sternberg and Glück (2021) describe in more detail why wisdom is so important as a wholesome ego-transcending value to develop, in our family, our work and our society. They explore how analytical thinking untempered by wisdom can be dangerous, how important it is in a global world to be comfortable with different viewpoints and how humanity needs to take a long hard look at reward systems so they do not encourage toxic behaviour and polarisation.[8]

Four key relational qualities for mindful communication

In this introductory chapter, we would also like to look at the four qualities that are key to mindful communication: kindness, compassion, sympathetic joy and equanimity. They can all four be developed as key relational qualities that help us engage with others and with ourselves in a wise and compassionate way. In Buddhism, they are referred to as the four Noble Abidings. In the secular training Mindfulness-Based Compassionate Living (MBCL), developed 15 years ago by Erik van den Brink and myself (Frits Koster), we refer to these qualities as the 'Four Friends for Life' (2015, 2018). They shift the focus from the ego system to the ecosystem, from 'Me First' or 'You First' to 'We Together'. Feldman (2017) refers to their practice as cultivating a boundless heart embracing all beings – past, present and future, near and far.

To illustrate these qualities, it might be helpful to think of a teacher and how she engages with different children in her class.

- She has a basic attitude of *kindness*. She wants all her pupils to be happy and to do well.
- She shows her *sympathetic joy* to those children who are successful, using their talents and flourishing.
- She turns with *compassion* towards those who have learning difficulties, poor health, problems at home or special needs.
- There may also be children whose behaviour is challenging or even anti-social (when they bully others and play truant). Her attitude towards those children might then be characterised by *equanimity*. She contains her own emotions as well as theirs, sets limits and stands firm. She does not accept unhealthy or harmful behaviour but nevertheless wishes them well and offers adequate space for them to learn.

Each of these relational qualities can be considered to be a type of 'medicine' when we find ourselves being sucked into their opposites that trouble our communications with others. Kindness is a remedy against hatred. Compassion can be a healthy response in the face of cruelty. Sympathetic joy can protect us against feeling envy and equanimity can prevent us from over-involvement or arrogance. These four qualities help us keep the right balance in our practice and avoid the pitfalls of one-sidedness. For instance, if we notice feeling overburdened by the heaviness of suffering, it can do us good to allow more lightness in the practice with loving kindness or sympathetic joy. If we lose our balance because we are too anxious or too eager, or strong emotions overwhelm us, we can practise equanimity. If we notice boredom or indifference, we may return to cultivating compassion or sympathetic joy. Mindfulness can help us attune to what may be most needed at each moment, in relation to ourselves and/or in relation to others.

Mindful attunement

All meditative traditions confirm that wisdom and the four friends for life can be developed by practising mindfulness, by non-judgementally being aware of an experience as an experience, in real time as it is experienced. The concept of 'mindful attunement' is nowadays often expressed as the ability to skilfully focus our attention intrapersonally – on our inner experiences – and interpersonally – in our relationships with others. Practice makes us more skilful. We describe six valuable communication programmes below which can teach us the art of mindful communication. In all these programmes mindfulness, wisdom and the four friends for life play an important role.

Nonviolent Communication

Of all the communication programmes mentioned in this book, Nonviolent Communication is probably the best known. It offers very practical tools and guidelines for a more skilful way of communicating. For example, we can learn how to name our observations of how other people behave and how this affects us emotionally, we can learn to express our own needs and ask for better cooperation. The founder was the American psychologist Marshall B. Rosenberg (1934–2015). It was his intention to use Nonviolent Communication to help people relate to each other better and to bring them to a deeper mutual respect and greater empowerment. The programme is taught in many settings and has been proved to be very effective, especially in major conflicts. We asked Oren Jay Sofer to write Chapter 2 of this book about Nonviolent Communication together with Sietske de Haan. Sofer teaches meditation and Nonviolent Communication internationally, he is the author of several books, including *Say what you mean* (2018). For many years now, De Haan has been counselling doctors and business leaders who are looking for a healthier way of living and working. She works with mindfulness, compassion and the principles of Nonviolent Communication.

Insight Dialogue

In 2006 and 2007, we took part in two Insight Dialogue retreats, and through this method developed by Kramer (2007, 2020), we became familiar with six practical guidelines for 'practising meditation in dialogue'. These guidelines include: *Pause, Relax, Open, Attune to Emergence, Speak the Truth and Listen Deeply.* Using these guidelines, specific areas of life, such as desire or impermanence, can be explored in pairs and larger groups.

This 'meditating in dialogue' turns out to be very revealing and enlightening. Through the practice of these six guidelines, we can become aware of all kinds of inner patterns and emotions, which can remain hidden in traditional silent retreats. Practising with the six guidelines provides a very practical and safe structure with which we can learn to integrate the practice of mindfulness into communication with others. In addition, these guidelines appear to offer enormous support to trainers, coaches, social workers and other professionals who work with people, in order to arrive at a way of communicating and supporting clients that consume less energy and are more effective.

From Insight Dialogue to Interpersonal Mindfulness

Insight Dialogue does have a clear Buddhist undertone and uses themes and terms that clearly refer to Buddhist philosophy. During practice, for example, people talk about 'hungers', 'suffering' and 'obstacles'. We were very pleased to hear that two leading mindfulness trainers from the USA, Florence Meleo-Meyer and Phyllis Hicks, with Kramer's permission, had designed a non-religious programme based on the principles of Insight Dialogue. This training is called the Interpersonal Mindfulness Program (IMP) and applies the six guidelines of the original programme into secular domains of work, such as health and education. We have invited psychiatrist and psychotherapist Erik van den Brink to describe the IMP in Chapter 3. Van den Brink has co-authored *Mindfulness-Based Compassionate Living* (2015) and *A practical guide to Mindfulness-Based Compassionate Living* (2018), which describe the MBCL programme he developed with Frits Koster. He is trained as an IMP teacher by Florence Meleo-Meyer and Phyllis Hicks.

Green Zone Communication

In our search for other programmes in which mindful communication is central, we discovered the work of Susan Gillis Chapman (2012). She was trained in Tibetan Buddhism and developed another non-religious communication programme based on the Shambhala tradition, which has been called Green Zone Communication, for several years now. This programme highlights very different aspects of communication from those mentioned above. For example, Gillis Chapman uses a model with three traffic lights, where communication can be called 'green' when it is flowing, 'yellow' when it becomes tense and 'red' when communication is jammed. She retired a few years ago and passed the baton to Greg Heffron. We asked Greg Heffron, Esther Hasselman and Chris Trani to devote Chapter 4 to the Green Zone programme. Heffron is the current Executive Director of Green Light Communication and he developed and teaches the Advanced Certification and Teacher Training courses to become a Green Zone teacher. Hasselman is the first Dutch-certified Green Zone trainer and a dedicated mindfulness practitioner, and she has also trained in other mindful communication programmes. Trani is a very experienced communication coach, consultant and facilitator and certified Green Zone trainer.

Mindfulness and Communication

We got to know the Flemish psychiatrist and mindfulness trainer Edel Maex (2014) during our own MBSR teacher training. We were immediately charmed by his mild, invitational approach and by the wonderfully poetic Flemish language with which he became one of the most famous mindfulness trainers in the Netherlands and Belgium. Maex has established a 'Mindfulness and Communication' course, in which he explores other aspects of mindful communication. One of the refreshing starting points is that we can never know exactly what is going on inside someone else, but we can be curious about that. We were delighted when Maex declared himself willing to take on Chapter 5.

Deep Listening

In 2016, we discovered Rosamund Oliver, a Scottish psychologist who has been increasingly successful in setting up a programme for people who work with people and want to develop their listening skills. In Deep Listening, we learn to listen with an open mind and from a physical listening centre without having to react directly. Many healthcare practitioners appear to be attracted to Deep Listening. We invited Rosamund Oliver and Chantal Bergers to write Chapter 6 together. Oliver founded the ACDLT® Deep Listening Training in 2003 and teaches it in many countries, Bergers has been working as a doctor and trainer for palliative care professionals for many years. She has been actively involved in the Awareness Centred Deep Listening Training (ACDLT) in the Netherlands from the outset and is a registered senior trainer of the programme.

Open Dialogue

A final programme that aroused our interest is Open Dialogue. This approach has its origins in the work of psychologist and psychotherapist Jaakko Seikkula and his multidisciplinary team at the Keropudas Hospital in Tornio, Finland (Seikkula and Arnkil, 2006). They deal with people who are experiencing a psychological crisis in a very inspirational and democratic way. Seikkula and his team not only involve the client, but also family members and other important people in the client's network, and organise meetings with this whole network. In the Netherlands, Open Dialogue, which is now officially called Peer-supported Open Dialogue (POD), offers a radical new approach. We asked Russell Razzaque, Heleen Wadman, psychiatrists Olaf Galisch and Kwok Hung Wong to devote a chapter to Open Dialogue. Razzaque (2014, 2019) has been a practising psychiatrist in the UK for over 20 years. He is currently an Associate Medical Director and Director of Research in his organisation, with Mindfulness and Open Dialogue as special fields of interest. Wadman experienced psychiatry as a client for many years. She has been using the experience with recovery she gained as a client, and her experience with mental healthcare as a peer worker and policy officer, within the mental healthcare system. Galisch has worked as a psychiatrist and medical director for many years. He has been involved in the development of Peer-supported Open Dialogue (POD) in the Netherlands since 2016; Hung Wong works as a mindfulness teacher and as a psychiatrist in Eindhoven and is a member of the first POD team in the Netherlands.

All the programmes in this book have aspects which overlap, but they also have unique characteristics, themes and perspectives. They are all intended to help us become more skilful in the complex world of living together and practising the art of mindful communication – intrapersonally and interpersonally.

Table 1.1 Resources

RESOURCES

Books:

- Erik van den Brink and Frits Koster (2015). *Mindfulness-Based Compassionate Living. A new training programme to deepen mindfulness with heartfulness.* London: Routledge.
- Erik van den Brink and Frits Koster, with Victoria Norton (2018). *A practical guide to Mindfulness-Based Compassionate Living. Living with heart.* London: Routledge.
- Joan Halifax (2019). *Standing at the edge: Finding freedom where fear and courage meet.* New York, NY: St. Martin's Press.
- Christopher Germer and Ronald Siegel (editors, 2014). *Compassion and wisdom in psychotherapy. Deepening mindfulness in clinical practice.* New York, NY: Guilford Press.
- Robert Sternberg and Judith Glück (2021). *Wisdom. The psychology of wise thoughts, words, and deeds.* Cambridge: University Press.

Audios:

- 1. Kindness Meditation – Yourself (Frits Koster).
- 2. Kindness Meditation – Self and Others (Frits Koster).
- See https://community.mindfulness-network.org/course/view.php?id=15 for basic mindfulness exercises.

Websites:

- www.fritskoster.com – website with information about activities by Frits Koster and Jetty Heynekamp.
- www.compassionateliving.info – website Frits Koster about the Mindfulness-Based Compassionate Living or MBCL training programme.
- www.mbcl.org – website Erik van den Brink about the Mindfulness-Based Compassionate Living or MBCL training programme.

Notes

1 From Paul Gilbert's foreword in *Mindfulness-Based Compassionate Living* by Erik van den Brink and Frits Koster (Routledge, 2015).
2 See www.compassionateliving.info, www.mbcl.org or www.mbcl-international.net for more information on this training.
3 See www.mentalhealth-uk.org/burnout.

4 For more information on compassion see the first two books in the resources table in this chapter.

5 See, e.g. the interview with Kabat-Zinn by the Omega Institute *How mindfulness can shape our collective future* on www.eomega.org/article/how-mindfulness-can-shape-our-collective-future.

6 See www.aau.at/en/blog/the-rocky-road-to-wisdom for an interview with Judith Glück.

7 This does not mean that wisdom would always need to have a long period of thinking and reflecting. Wisdom can also arise spontaneously. But at least we allow ourselves the space to reflect when there is time and necessity for this, e.g. in the case of a dilemma needing more time.

8 In the UK, mindfulness teacher Annie Akasati McAuley and mindfulness teacher and researcher Carolyn Drake have developed an interesting eight-week mindfulness-based programme exploring many facets of wisdom in a secular. It is called Mindfulness-Based Wise Awareness (MBWA). See www.lovemindfulness.co.uk/wise-awareness/ and see www.evidencebasedwisdom.com/ for more information on evidence-based wisdom.

Chapter 2

Nonviolent Communication
Mindfulness and compassion in relationships

Oren Jay Sofer and Sietske de Haan

> *There is space between stimulus and response. In that space lies our ability to choose a response. In that response lies our growth and freedom.*
> attributed to Viktor Frankl

Introduction

In this chapter, we give a brief overview of what mindfulness is and some secular applications like the eight-week training Mindfulness-Based Stress Reduction (MBSR). We explain the model of Nonviolent Communication (NVC), and how training in mindfulness and NVC complement each other.

This is followed by a summary of key elements of programmes we developed, where mindfulness and NVC are combined. You will also find some exercises to get started and learn about the experiences of people who have already participated in the training.

We hope that this chapter will provide you with some insight and tools which you can apply directly in your work and your private life. We also hope that the effects of this chapter (and indeed this whole book) may contribute to more compassion and connection between people and in our world.

A moment of awareness is a small pause. It may seem insignificant at first, but it is within this space of a pause that we can choose compassion and connection, that we can change our life or the life of another person completely, and that we can work together to create a different world.

How we came to this work

Both of us (Sietske and Oren) discovered NVC after a number of years of formal, intensive meditation practice. In our own way, we each noticed a longing for a more whole-hearted and complete integration of the values of our meditation practice into our day-to-day lives, relationships and conversations.

DOI: 10.4324/9781003262008-2

In conversation with each other, we found remarkable parallels in our personal journey. We were both experiencing the benefits of meditation – more awareness, less reactivity, greater connection with qualities like compassion, kindness and patience. Yet, we also noticed that it was still challenging to stay aware in conversation with others.

Oren: 'Working in a fast-paced environment as a cook at a meditation retreat centre, I noticed how quickly the values of compassion and understanding would evaporate when there was a disagreement with a fellow cook! The perspective and qualities of the meditation were even less accessible in tense, highly habituated interactions with close family members.'

Sietske: 'I noticed how difficult it was not to get lost in the moment. In my enthusiasm, I could often be too quick. At other times, I noticed the tendency to withdraw or shut down emotionally if the other person came on more strongly than I felt comfortable with.'

Noticing these gaps in our spiritual practice, we each felt a longing to embody in all moments – even the deeply stimulating ones – the values we held so dear, like connection, love, mutual understanding, curiosity and equity. We each feel fortunate to have discovered NVC, a communication model developed by Marshall Rosenberg (1934–2015).

As we each began to learn the practice of NVC (sometimes referred to as 'Compassionate Communication' in English, or 'Connected Communication' in Dutch), we noticed differences between people with and without meditation experience. Some of the core components of NVC are:

1. Cultivating a particular view of human nature and behaviour.
2. Developing a strong intention to build understanding and connection.
3. Training one's attention to clearly identify emotions and underlying human needs.

In each of these areas, we have noticed in ourselves and through training thousands of students, that those with previous meditation experience had an easier time understanding, integrating and applying the NVC model. Based on humanistic psychology, NVC suggests that all humans share the same underlying, universal needs and that all actions and behaviours can be seen and understood as an attempt to meet those needs. We practice shifting out of habitual views like 'who's right and who's wrong,' or what 'should or shouldn't have happened' and instead viewing a situation from the perspective of the various needs at stake. What does each person ultimately care about? Can we connect with some deeper layer of our shared humanity? Those with meditation training (or other forms of spiritual or contemplative practice) were often less wedded to their views of right and wrong and had stronger access to the compassionate view that all humans are longing for some kind of fulfilment of needs.

Similarly, those with meditation (or similar) training were generally more able to shift out of habitual energies of blame, defensiveness, or control and into a stance of genuine curiosity. These shifts in view (human needs) and intention (to become curious and connect) form an essential internal basis of the practice of NVC.

This internal basis is supported by training one's attention to identify specific aspects of our own and others' experience – most notably the feelings and needs that are present in any situation. Again, anecdotally, we noticed that meditators tended to have a higher degree of self-awareness, more developed sensory perception and greater access to both cognitive understanding and somatic experience of their feelings and needs.

A family doctor who followed a module of NVC in a retreat for doctors told Sietske the following a few months after the retreat:

> I had a patient today who felt that he had not been heard by the doctor yesterday, and he kept on talking. He was frightened and thought that something was very wrong and he had to be rushed to the hospital. I tried to ask him questions, but I couldn't get through. I noticed that I was getting angry and tried to shout at him. But suddenly I realised that…and I could stop myself. Thanks to what I learned, I noticed earlier than usual that I was completely absorbed in the patient's emotions and reaction. At that moment I realised that I had a choice and did not have to go along with his dynamics. Then I sat back and became quiet. I looked at him calmly and called him by his name in a very friendly way, and then he was more in the moment, there was more connection. I was then able to name what I saw happening to him, and we really started talking again.

Who is Nonviolent Communication for?

Though one may think of communication skills as being specifically relevant in situations of conflict, communication is at the centre of our lives as human beings. We communicate all day long and the quality of our communication determines, to a significant degree, the quality of our relationships and effectiveness in life. These skills, therefore, have a wide range of applications in all areas of human life, from our relationship with ourselves, our own emotional, psychological and spiritual lives, to our relationships with others personally and professionally, to our lives as citizens and social beings.

We may have trouble being aware of our own feelings or needs, or experience unease in connecting with people or find ourselves often caught up in conflict. If we are not able to skilfully deal with difficult emotions and difficult communication, it can have a great impact on our work and private life, so there is much to be gained by learning these skills. If we become curious about what is going on inside ourselves and are open to wholeheartedly listening to others it can bring about inner healing and healing of relationships, deeper connections, better cooperation and harmonious living together. These training programs are especially valuable for those who communicate a lot in their work, such as care providers.

NVC is also a powerful tool in working for social change. Founder Dr. Marshall Rosenberg (2005, 2015) named the practice 'Nonviolent Communication' specifically to place it within the tradition of Kingian and Gandhian Nonviolence. He saw this as a powerful and essential ingredient in movements working for social transformation. On an immediate level, developing one's skills for clear communication can support us to be more effective organisers – communicating with constituents, running meetings and building coalitions more robustly. The skills can also help us to negotiate more powerfully by helping to create the conditions for more mutual understanding, alignment, purpose and human connection.

On a broader level, Rosenberg's analysis of the origins of social inequality and oppression includes our language and thoughts as a key component in the perpetuation of dysfunctional (and often violent) social institutions. His analysis highlights four key areas that create and maintain current social structures:

- Our underlying theory of human nature, which informs.
- The social structures we create, which help determine.
- Systems of education and socialisation, which in turn influences.
- Human behaviour, that eventually confirms and reinforces our views of human nature.

Each aspect influences and informs the other three in complex feedback loops. When we view human nature as selfish and greedy (based on human history and the personal experiences of human behaviour we have), we will create social structures like punitive justice and incentive-based economics. Educational systems and the socialisation process will all prepare children to live in a world defined by attempts to win, get ahead and protect one's own.

The practice of NVC provides a different vision of human nature and society – one based on our potential for compassion, generosity and creative collaboration – and a practice to embody that vision. Working for social change, without shifting the underlying basis of our consciousness and the ways we communicate, runs the risk of recreating the very dynamics of oppression and inequality we want to change. This is because our views, unconscious habits and language help to create and reinforce social structures.

Today, there are certain critiques of NVC as unintentionally reinforcing the dominant social paradigm of oppression by prioritising the experiences and views of those who identify as white or from the Global North. Given how far this is from the intention and vision of NVC, many practitioners and teachers of NVC today are actively exploring what aspects of these critiques may be valid and how to make the training and tools of NVC as relevant as possible to people from all classes, social and economic positions. Part of this exploration includes examining how our own unconscious views, or life experiences, can influence how we learn, apply and teach NVC. For example, as a male, Oren will be less aware of the unique challenges faced by women, trans or non-binary individuals. Based on our gender and the roles we've been assigned by society, we often face different challenges in identifying our feelings and needs. By actively learning about these differences and becoming aware of any assumptions we carry, we can share these skills in more relevant and accessible ways. The same holds true for other aspects of our identity and life experience in terms of race, class, sexual orientation, ability and more.

The relevance of mindfulness

Mindfulness is the capacity to pay attention to our present moment experience in a balanced, open and curious way. It is an innate capacity that all humans have, and one that can be actively cultivated. The modern, Western understanding of mindfulness and many of the techniques for strengthening it comes from Buddhist traditions in South and Southeast Asia. As practitioners, we both deeply honour the historical and cultural roots of mindfulness in Buddhist practice.

In the late 20th century, individuals like Jon Kabat-Zinn, Daniel Goleman and Richard Davidson, helped to create the modern movement of secular mindfulness. John Kabat-Zinn conducted the first clinical trials on the benefits of mindfulness practice for those with chronic pain, which later led to the codification of what has become known as Mindfulness Based Stress Reduction (MBSR). As both clinical and neuroscientific research expanded, mindfulness practices began to become integrated into other sectors of modern society, most notably the mental health and education fields.

Mindfulness plays a key role in the transformation of consciousness because of its capacity to illuminate the habits and patterns of the mind in a balanced and non-judgemental way. Mindfulness helps to reveal underlying tendencies in our thoughts, beliefs and emotions, and ways of being, and creates the possibility of understanding what is truly for our own welfare and the welfare of others, and what is hindering our growth and well-being. Part of what makes this possible is the ability of mindfulness to weaken, or decondition states of mind that, when unchecked, produce suffering in ourselves and the world (such as greed, hatred and ignorance) and to strengthen qualities of mind that support human thriving (such as kindness, generosity and wisdom). Further, as we have noted above, the power of mindfulness to enhance cognitive, emotional and sensory awareness provides an indispensable support for communication training.

Mindfulness-Based Stress Reduction

There are many different forms and systems of mindfulness training. MBSR, as developed by Jon Kabat-Zinn, is loosely based on a traditional sequence of instructions for cultivating awareness known as 'satipatthana vipassana,' from the Buddhist Theravada school of Buddhism in Myanmar known in the lineage of Mahasi Sayadaw. We will use the template of MBSR training here to describe the cultivation of mindfulness, with the recognition that there are many other valid forms of the practice.

The value of training mindfulness

In the eight-week MBSR training, participants learn to become more mindful in their daily lives through various awareness exercises. They learn to live less on automatic pilot and to regularly pause and become aware of what can be experienced here and now. It helps people to get a better view of their reality and what is needed. They discover the moments when they slip into automatic reactions in their thinking and behaviour. By investigating with compassion when and how they get stuck or sabotage themselves, space is created for other choices and for finding ways to fulfil needs in a healthy way. They develop more self-compassion and start to feel more clearly where their limits and possibilities lie.

Mindfulness as the basis for NVC

In the first weeks of the MBSR training, participants practice becoming progressively aware of the body, the breath, feelings, thoughts and everything that comes through the senses. There are a variety of meditation exercises, reflections and writing assignments. For example, one assignment invites participants to investigate for a week what happens when you experience something pleasant and what happens when you experience something unpleasant. Becoming aware of this 'pleasant or unpleasant' valence, what's known as the feeling tone of a sensation or experience, has great potential to yield insight, freedom and choice. We usually react automatically by pushing unpleasant experiences away or judging them, and holding on to pleasant experiences and wanting more of them. This way of relating to pleasure and pain does not always make us happier. It takes a great deal of mental energy and does not always have the desired outcome. By learning to stop and experience what is there with kindness and not reacting for a moment, we start to see new possibilities.

Up to halfway through the training, the focus is mainly on stressful moments, where we react automatically. By opening to feeling the discomfort in such difficult moments, participants learn to be responsive instead of reactive, as the family doctor shared in the above example. Mindfulness provides a basis for becoming more aware of what happens in and around you, and what reactions this evokes in you, without having to judge or interpret these directly. This increasing awareness can help us to take responsibility for our life with wisdom and care.

NVC provides extra structure and clarity to put this responsibility into practice, both in communication with yourself and with others. After all, in both MBSR and NVC you ask the same questions: 'What exactly is happening here? What do I really need? And does my choice enrich my life or is it harmful?'

The form and spirit of NVC

As we begin to explore the practices and tools of NVC, we want to differentiate between the technique itself and its underlying ethos or intention. NVC is designed to help us to have more clarity, awareness and flexibility personally, and to communicate in ways that foster greater understanding, connection and collaboration. All of the tools, practices and techniques are strategies to serve these aims.

One of the dangers in any systematic training is that the practitioner will become overly focused on the technique to the detriment of its underlying aims. Human communication is complex, nuanced and entirely context-sensitive. Every situation is different. To use the tools of NVC as intended requires that we apply them intelligently, relying on our own intuition, wisdom and life experience to gauge what will be the most authentic and supportive way to create the conditions for more understanding and collaboration.

As trainer Kit Miller (former Director of Bay Area NVC and the Gandhi Institute) once said: 'Nonviolent Communication is an awareness discipline masquerading as a communication technique.' At its heart, NVC supports a profound transformation of our consciousness, one in which we shift from viewing the world through the lens of separation, scarcity and powerlessness to a world of interdependence, flow and human resourcefulness. We shift out of thinking in binary systems of right and wrong, should and shouldn't, either or, to holding a dynamic trust in shared humanity and creative solutions; from habits of blame, reactive judgement and defensiveness, to more conscious intentions of curiosity, compassion and collaboration.

One of the key insights of Dr. Rosenberg was that this transformation of consciousness is supported by training our attention to focus on four specific aspects of human experience that make it easier to stay connected to compassion and a sense of our shared humanity:

- Observations
- Feelings
- Needs
- Requests

Formal training in NVC generally focuses on increasing awareness of these four, key components, along with certain core intentions (curiosity, compassion and collaboration) and orientations to dialogue (self-connection, empathic listening and honest self-expression).

When integrating mindfulness into NVC, we often begin the training by encouraging students to cultivate a foundation of self-awareness. This can be done in a variety of ways, through formal mindfulness practice, MBSR training, as well as various other awareness disciplines.

Within our approach, cultivating somatic (embodied) awareness offers a range of powerful benefits, with certain cautions required as well in order to make the practice safe and accessible to all. Some of the benefits of embodied awareness include:

- Increased space for connection and mutuality relationally (others can tell when we are present).
- Better access to self-regulation skills.
- More information about one's own feelings, needs and thoughts.
- More information about the other person's feelings, needs and thoughts.
- Increased awareness of one's habit patterns and reactivity.
- Earlier detection of defensiveness and emotional reactivity.
- Stronger capacity to tolerate the discomfort of emotional reactivity.
- More tools to integrate and channel the energy of defensiveness or reactivity.

As mammals, embodied, present-time awareness is a natural and innate capacity for human beings. However, as we grow up and are socialised, as we develop strategies to cope with the pressure and demands of life, many of us lose touch with this ability to be aware of our body and environment in a grounded and connected manner. Therefore, it takes some time to redevelop this capacity to rest our attention in the body.

For those who have experienced trauma, becoming aware of sensations in the body can bring up strong feelings or disturbing memories from the past. For this reason, it's essential that those teaching somatic awareness skills have some training in trauma-sensitive approaches. This often includes offering basic psycho-education about how nervous system activation and self-regulation work, along with some tools for grounding and resourcing. These include orienting (connecting to one's environment through the senses, often practised by visually scanning the room or space in a relaxed and curious way); placing attention in the extremities of the body (hands and/or feet); or thinking of a good friend, a mentor, or a comforting place from one's life as a way of bringing more ease and safety into the nervous system. When doing introductory somatic exercises, we often remind participants that they are welcome to keep their eyes open if they prefer, or to open their eyes and look around if they begin to feel overwhelmed at any point.

There are many additional tools for developing somatic awareness. MBSR training uses a body scan meditation and mindful yoga. Other techniques include awareness of the breath and meditating on body sensations. (In the first chapter by Frits Koster, Jetty Heynekamp and Victoria Norton, you can find a link to a body scan meditation.)

Training exercises

In this section, we share instructions for specific exercises you can do to explore cultivating mindfulness and integrating it into your communication practice.

Exercise: Cultivating relational awareness

Relational awareness is the ability to be aware of oneself and another person at the same time. It's an essential foundation for conversation and an advanced skill that builds on somatic awareness. To help participants begin to cultivate relational awareness during conversations, we may invite them to practise in pairs with a simple exercise of speaking and listening. We begin from silence, inviting each person to do a short body scan and to become generally aware of the sensations in their body from head to toe. This helps to establish somatic awareness individually before connecting relationally.

We then invite them to open their eyes and notice if they're able to maintain an awareness of internal bodily sensations as they see one another. Many participants often comment on how quickly they lose awareness as soon as they are in visual contact with another person! From here, we invite the speaker to share two or three simple pieces of information (such as their name, where they live and what they ate for breakfast) while trying to stay aware of a sensation in their body like their hands in the lap. The listener is invited to listen silently, also attempting to maintain a small amount of embodied awareness. After the first person shares, we return to silence and again support participants to connect fully with their bodies, noticing what it was like to speak or listen with awareness. Participants then trade roles and repeat the exercise.

Finally, we invite participants to release the form of having a 'speaker' and 'listener' and discuss what they each noticed – again, attempting to stay lightly aware of a sensation in their body as they speak or listen. Many participants report having powerful insights from this simple exercise: from noticing how much anxiety drives their communication, to uncovering other habits that may be influencing their relationships.

The basic structure of this exercise can be repeated to practice other tools for developing relational awareness in conversation such as pausing, modulating one's pace of speech, anchoring one's attention in the space between the two parties, or the space around both parties.

Compassion and curiosity

Earlier we wrote that the shifts in view (human needs) and intention (to get curious and connect) form an essential basis of the practice of NVC. Exploring what each person ultimately cares about, opens us to connect from a place of compassion. Deeply realising we all want to feel safe, healthy, happy and at ease brings us into connection at the level of our shared humanity. Even if we are having a difficult moment with someone, remembering that we all try to take care of our needs can help us to connect with curiosity and care.

Exercise: Compassion and curiosity

Loving-kindness meditation offers another way to practice this formally. The meditation starts with wishing oneself or another: may I/you be safe, may I/you be happy, may I/you be healthy, may I/you be at ease. Start where it's easiest for you. The practice then continues by expanding the benevolent wishes to others, in widening circles. First, extending the wish to friends and people that are dear to you, then to people you have a more neutral relationship with, and if your practice gets stronger, eventually wishing well to people you have conflicts with (there is a link to a short metta or loving-kindness meditation at the end of this chapter).

After a mindfulness and NVC retreat a medical specialist became more aware of how important and difficult it is to be consciously present in a conversation. He said that he always had a rather pithy style of communicating, and that this often led to fights in the team. After the training he said: 'I notice that I now ramble less, and am more curious about what colleagues and nurses think, I now want to know more often what their ideas are. Still, I often get caught up in the madness of the day and want to do too much too soon. When I see that everyone is dragging their heels, I know that I have to stop. Then sometimes I go back to the list in my head from the *metta* or loving-kindness meditation and wish myself and others love and safety and health and happiness. I also do this during operations, and it brings a lot of peace. In meetings, it neutralises the atmosphere, takes the sting out of it and I can ask myself: 'What am I doing? What are we doing now?'

Exercise: Unmet needs

Here is another short practice you can do on your own: when someone is mad at you, see if you can remember the essential view that all of us are trying to meet fundamental, shared needs. Then, see if you can stretch your heart with empathy and get curious: what unmet need(s) could the other person have?

Seeing judgements as a source of information

In mindfulness practice, and also in the first component of NVC, one practices observing without judging. However, we may soon discover that paradoxically we are constantly judging! These judgements can also be used as a source of information about what is important to you in the service of more discernment and compassion. As you continue to practice NVC, you will find that even with this exercise in mind, it will become easier to recognise the underlying needs people are trying to express when they make judgements. Here is one exercise we use for this.

Exercise: Transforming judgements to compassion and understanding

Before reading on, think of a judgement about yourself or another person. Then go through the following steps:

What was the event or observation that preceded this judgement? What exactly happened? What did someone say or do? Judgements are often fuelled by interpretation, comparison, or classification.

What feelings have been stirred up in you? How does that affect you? Try to become aware of your emotions as you experience them directly, rather than the thoughts or interpretations that colour them (see below on 'quasi-feelings').

What need has been touched here? What is important to you here? Can you connect fully with how valuable this need is to you?

What ideas might you have for satisfying this need, or addressing the situation? What action would you like to take regarding yourself or someone else?

Negative judgements are usually about unmet needs, and positive judgements are about met needs. Participants of the NVC training regularly use this exercise, and both of us do some form of it regularly. When we gain insight into what is in us and become aware of what is important to us, it helps to take care of what you need in a clear, healthy and direct way. Judgement also makes things static, and when you peel away the judgement and uncover the underlying feelings and needs, things can start moving again.

Observation

The first component of training attention in NVC is learning to observe clearly. This means observing and describing a situation as factually as possible. We practise being aware when interpretations, judgements, generalisations and other secondary reactions are added. When we notice this, we go back to our description of what happened to a direct and as factual as possible observation.

Exercise: Observation

A practice to do alone or with a friend is writing down a situation that is stimulating for you, or where you have strong emotions (not too strong, so you can stay balanced and learn from the exercise). Then read back to yourself or the other carefully and see if it is an observation or where it is mixed with interpretations or judgements. Whenever you notice interpretations, try to become more clear and specific about the actual observations.

Another practice involves walking around the room three times: the first time coming from an angry state of mind, the second time from a happy state of mind, and the third time as factually as possible and in the here and now. How does each state of mind affect your experience of seeing the room? How do you walk? How do you breathe? What do you see?

This exercise only takes a few minutes. In the early years of this training, Sietske worked in a beautiful monumental building with painted ceilings and beautiful wood carvings, so there was a lot to see. The first time the participants did this exercise, walking around in an angry state of mind, they saw that one crack in the ceiling, the 'messiness' of all the training stuff, the irregularity of the old wooden floor and the 'strange' arm on the painting above the stove. The second time, they saw how the light shone through the crystals of the chandelier, the colourfulness of the painting and so on. And the third time, they perceived the environment much more factually, with fewer judgements – positive or negative. People regularly said that they had actually seen a different room three times. They also noticed that in the angry pose, they looked down more on average, and also more often with a narrowed view. In the third posture, they looked around more openly and were able to observe more easily without judgement or interpretation.

If we are aware of the way in which our feelings, states of mind and thoughts can colour our gaze, this can provide a great deal of clarity. A family doctor once remarked beautifully: 'If I find the first four patients in my surgery annoying, I must have got up on the wrong side of the bed.'

Feelings

We live in an interdependent world where events, actions and words affect us. When something happens or we observe something, quite often we feel something about it. Feelings are the second component of Rosenberg's model. Rosenberg looked very carefully at the words we use when we talk about feelings. He made a distinction between feelings and 'quasi-feelings.' Feelings are defined as the actual emotions we experience in our body, distinct from any interpretation, judgement, or narrative about another person. Examples of feelings are relaxed, anxious, angry, sad, gloomy, happy, open and grateful. Feelings of abandonment, manipulation, pressure, threat and rejection fall into the category of quasi-feelings; they imply judgement or blame of the other person. In effect, they suggest 'You're doing this to me,' often saying more about how we interpret events than about what kind of feeling we are actually experiencing.

For example, if one feels 'abandoned' – a genuine experience many of us have had – we are on one level telling ourselves: 'This person abandoned me.' What emotions are present? We might feel hurt, alone, devastated, confused, angry, shocked... There is such a wide range of feelings that may be present connected to this general description of 'abandoned.' If we were to discuss the situation with the other person, which description of our feelings is more likely to lead to connection? Which more likely to lead to defensiveness?

When you see yourself naming a quasi-feeling, it helps to explore further: how does that feel inside? Body awareness can help here to find words for feelings.

When coaching clients, the moment they go from a quasi-feeling to a feeling, often their breathing becomes deeper, and they often say with relief: 'Yes, that's how I feel.' For example, a woman recently talked about recurring conversations with a loved one in which the other person rarely asked her how she was. Somewhat flatly she said 'I don't feel seen and heard then.' When asked about her feelings, she took a deep breath. Her face lit up and she said clearly, 'I feel angry, because in a relationship I would like to be able to also tell my story.' Feelings are triggered by observation, or by what we think about that observation. Furthermore, it is very important to realise that the feeling that arises is not caused by the perception or event, but has to do with an underlying need that is present.

Feelings versus quasi-feelings

As described above, Rosenberg made a distinction between feelings and quasi-feelings. Here is part of the list he used as an example. Note the two columns in Table 2.1 do not correspond with one another. That is, the feelings on the right are not translations of the quasi-feelings on the left, but rather are offered as examples.

When we are exploring feelings, this is an exercise you can do to become familiar with a greater wealth of words for feelings and to learn to distinguish when we name feelings or quasi-feelings. Participants choose a situation from their lives and explore what they felt then. Often the feeling comes back while remembering. In pairs, participants search for words for a feeling when quasi-feelings are named, and learn to notice the difference in experience when a word for a feeling is found. Participants usually notice that when they name a quasi-feeling, they experience more distance, and when they name a feeling, they experience more connection. Try this out with the following exercise.

Exercise: Exploring feelings

Think back to a conflict or a conversation with someone that was slightly difficult, preferably a conversation that you can still remember clearly. Find a moment in the conversation when you experienced an important or painful feeling. (But not so painful that you become overwhelmed just by remembering it.) What exactly do you feel when you think back to that moment? Tune in to your body. The word you choose, is it a feeling or a quasi-feeling? And if you discover it is a quasi-feeling, what is underneath? How do you feel on the inside? Do you notice any difference when using a word that expresses a feeling and a word that expresses a quasi-feeling?

Sometimes the difference between a quasi-feeling and an (underlying) feeling can be great, sometimes the differences are subtle. Try exploring this further yourself, and notice how it affects conversations with others.

Table 2.1 Quasi-feelings and feelings

Quasi-feelings	Feelings
Encouraged, affected, attacked, separated, rejected, threatened, deceived, helpful, used, charmed, hindered, intimidated, manipulated, tyrannised, distrusted, cornered, abandoned, condescended to, not heard, not supported, not valued, not wanted, not seen, not taken seriously, misunderstood, humiliated.	Breathless, alert, anxious, fearful, sad, depressed, comfortable, shaky, fearful, animated, happy, angry, bubbling, grumpy, grateful, overjoyed, terrified, lonely, miserable, energetic, ecstatic, lifeless, agitated, frustrated, irritated, happy, blissful, excited, touched, shocked, frightened, tense.

Needs

The third component of training awareness in Rosenberg's model is to become aware of needs. Needs are what is really important to us. We all share the same basic needs, such as safety, warmth, affection, food, sleep, rest, respect, inspiration, intimacy, creativity and expression, to name just a few. Conflicts with others (and with ourselves), usually arise at the level of how we want to satisfy those needs – what we refer to as 'strategies' in NVC. If, in a difficult conversation, we hear what the other person's underlying needs are and they can share what is important to them, what their needs are, this automatically increases empathy, understanding and connection. Then, more space is created to explore together whether a suitable and more mutually supportive solution to the needs can be found. Here is a short list of needs to give you a sense of what we mean (Table 2.2).

Table 2.2 Needs

Needs		
Appreciation	Contribution	Mourning
Authenticity	Dignity	Mutuality
Autonomy	Empathy	Peace
Balance	Freedom	Play
Beauty	Growth	Purpose
Belonging	Honesty	Rest
Choice	Learning	Self-expression
Companionship	Love	Sustenance
Consideration	Meaning	Touch

Exercise: Exploring your needs

Think of two needs and your habitual ways of fulfilling them. Then, for each need, think of a number of other ways of fulfilling these needs. Which gives better results? What do you gain by thinking of alternatives?

Another practice: choose one or two habits that are behavioural patterns that you don't like. Perhaps these habits don't benefit your health, relationships or peace of mind. Explore with compassion: what needs are underneath this habit? When you do this, what does it give you? Are there other strategies that could fulfil this need? And is there something other people could do to contribute?

Requests

The fourth component of training attention in Marshall Rosenberg's model is to consider how we can move a conversation forward by making a request. A *request* is a question designed to further the project of attending to all of the needs present. In some cases, it is a question that is aimed at gauging the willingness of another person to perform a specific action or task. Requests are meant to be specific, clear, doable and flexible. They're intended to build trust and collaboration rather than using coercion, force, blame, shame or manipulation to get things done. Any time we use our power to get someone to do something it comes at a cost: either in the relationship or in the quality of the outcomes.

Essentially, a request is a strategy to meet needs. It's a proposal we offer as a way forward in the moment that suggests, 'How about this? Here's what I think could be helpful right now; what do you think?' We can make requests designed to support more connection and understanding, checking if we're on the same page in the conversation. For example, 'Is this making sense?' will give us some information about how we're coming across to the other person and the degree of confidence they have that they understand what we're saying. 'How is it for you to hear all of this?' will give us more information about their internal response.

A simple way to practice requests is to think of a situation in which you want to discuss something with someone else. Then, think of at least three potential proposals for a way forward. On a concrete level, what would resolve this for you? Or, what would help to move the situation forward to the next stage? The more ideas you have for how to work things out, the more flexible you can be in the conversation. Then, for each strategy, formulate a request: how can you suggest this to the other person in a way that lets them know you'd like their input and want this to work for them too? Often, we might phrase a request by saying, 'How about...' or 'Could you...' or 'Would it work for you to...' or even, 'Would you be willing to...?'

Finally, for each request, check if it's specific rather than vague. For example, being a 'team player' is vague. Volunteering once a month to facilitate our team meeting is specific. Is it a positive, doable action rather than a negative. For example, 'Stop micromanaging me' is what you don't want. 'Could you tell me when you have questions or concerns about my work and ask how I'm handling something before giving me more instructions?' would be a positive request. Finally, check inside to see if the *spirit* of the question is flexible. Are you open to hearing 'no'? If not, then it doesn't matter how you ask – it will likely come across as a demand. Take time to reflect on what needs this other person has that might prevent them from saying yes as a way of moving beyond your own fixation on this particular strategy.

Exercise: Listening

One of the most powerful exercises for listening and speaking is often the simplest. Set up the form of speaker and listener as above, and invite people into a place of grounded, embodied awareness. Have the speaker share about something important to them in their life for 3–5 minutes, taking care to instruct them not to choose anything too challenging or emotionally disregulating. (The aim here is to learn a new skill, which is harder to do if we're flooded with emotions.)

The speaker can practice speaking with awareness, using any of the tools we've mentioned above for staying aware while speaking: grounding their attention in their body, pausing, or slowing down. Invite them to explore what it's like to take their time speaking, to choose their words with care, trusting that the other person won't interrupt and will just be listening silently.

Instruct the listeners to listen wholeheartedly, with curiosity and warmth. There's nothing they need to do, figure out, fix or solve. Simply listen to understand. Be sure to make it clear that the listener's role at this point is simply to listen silently. It's okay to make eye contact, to nod or allow natural nonverbal expressions to arise. However, the listener is discouraged from asking questions, giving advice, or responding in any way while the speaker is sharing.

Start from a place of silence, guiding the participants into a state of embodied awareness. Remind each person briefly of the skill they are practicing and the corresponding intention (for the listener, curiosity and warmth; for the speaker, to speak with awareness).

After 3–5 minutes have passed, ring a bell signalling that the time has ended and invite the participants back into silence. Then, guide the listeners to consider what matters most to the speaker. How do they feel? What's most important to them? (You are pointing them to identify needs, without needing to necessarily call it that.) Then, after they've had a few moments to consider this, have them take a guess or two about what matters most to the speaker. This should be in the form of a simple question: 'Is what matters to you most here...?' Or, 'Is what's important to you something about...?'

Finally, allow the speaker to respond authentically, briefly, for a minute or two. Return to silence, then trade roles and repeat. Finally, at the end, invite the pairs to discuss together what they learned or noticed.

Exercise: Speaking

One favourite exercise for bringing these tools into speaking involves the following steps:

- *Guide participants to reflect on what is true for them using the form/template of Observation – Feeling – Need – Request. Have them consider each component separately, for one specific part of a situation or conversation. What happened? How do you feel about it? Why/what matters to you? And, where would you like to go from here? What ideas or requests do you have? This is meant to be an internal reflection to prepare them for speaking by becoming clearer about what is true inside.*

- *Then, invite them to consider what they want to say to the other person. Without editing it or trying to even use these tools, what would you want to say if the person could hear it?*

- Next, point out that most of the time when we speak it's because we want to be understood. Ask them to consider next, 'What is it you'd like the other person to understand about you or your experience?' This changes the focus from what I want to say to what I want to be understood for, beginning to include an awareness of the listener and the message itself.
- Ask them to consider, 'How can you say this in a way that the other person is MOST likely to be able to understand or hear?' Remembering that we often speak to be understood, we can place our focus on how to increase the chances of that. One key here is trying to translate any blame or judgement into our direct experience of feelings and needs, which tends to reduce the chances the other person will become defensive.
- For the final part, have each person share this last piece with someone else in the group and get input on how it would be for them to hear this. Would they get defensive? Is it clear? Is there any blame or judgement in it? If so, how might they say it differently.

We have found that using the NVC format for prior reflection and then considering these direct questions can help people to translate the consciousness of NVC (of collaboration, nonviolence, care and compassion) into a more authentic form of self-expression.

Exercise: Transforming judgements to compassion and understanding

Before reading on, think of a judgement about yourself or another person. Then go through the following steps:

What was the event or observation that preceded this judgement? What exactly happened? What did someone say or do? Judgements are often fuelled by interpretation, comparison or classification.

What feelings have been stirred up in you? How does that affect you? Try to become aware of your emotions as you experience them directly, rather than the thoughts or interpretations that colour them (see below on quasi-feelings). What need has been touched here? What is important to you here? Can you connect fully with how valuable this need is to you? What ideas might you have for satisfying this need, or addressing the situation? What action would you like to take regarding yourself or someone else?

Negative judgements are usually about unmet needs, and positive judgements are about met needs. We ourselves and participants of the Nonviolent Communication training regularly use this exercise. When we gain insight into what is in us and become aware of what is important to us, it helps to take care of what we need in a clear, healthy and direct way. Judgement also makes things static, and when we peel away the judgement and uncover the underlying feelings and needs, things can start moving again.

Conclusion

We all come to this training and process with many years of conditioning. In our experience, it can take time and patience to shift such deeply ingrained habits as the way we communicate, but that this transformation is entirely possible for each and every one of us.

The need for more effective and compassionate communication is clear in so many areas of our world today – from the personal to the professional to the social realms. Skilful communication alone will not be sufficient to handle

Table 2.3 Resources

RESOURCES

Books:
- Miki Kashtan (2014). *Spinning threads of radical aliveness: Transcending the legacy of separation in our individual lives.* Auckland, New Zealand: Fearless Heart Publications.
- Lucy Leu (2015). *Nonviolent Communication companion workbook. A practical guide for individual, group, or classroom study.* Encinitas, CA: PuddleDancer Press.
- Marshall Rosenberg (2005). *Practical spirituality. Reflections on the spiritual basis of Nonviolent Communication.* Encinitas, CA: PuddleDancer Press.
- Marshall Rosenberg (2015). *Nonviolent communication: A language of life.* Louisville, CO: Sounds True.
- Oren Jay Sofer (2018). *Say what you mean: A mindful approach to Nonviolent Communication.* Boston, MA, Shambhala.

Audio:
- www.orenjaysofer.com/book-audio/

Video:
- www.youtube.com/orenjaysofervideo – Youtube channel with videos on Nonviolent Communication and guided meditation exercises by Oren Sofer.

Websites:
- www.orenjaysofer.com – website Oren Jay Sofer.
- www.baynvc.org – website BayNVC.
- www.cnvc.org – website Center for Nonviolent Communication.
- www.roxannemanning.com – website Roxy Manning.
- www.thefearlessheart.org – website Miki Kashtan.
- www.compassioninbusiness.com/english – website Sietske de Haan.
- www.gezondedokter.nl/english – website Sietske de Haan for doctors and other medical specialists.

the immense challenges we face as a species – from the climate crisis to the disintegration of the social fabric due to increased polarisation, from the gross inequities of resource distribution to the need for more understanding across differences. However, we will not be able to resolve them without more robust and intelligent ways of communicating. We believe that the world can benefit immensely from this training, and it is our hope that this chapter might play some small role in inspiring you to learn, practice and share these skills.

Chapter 3

Interpersonal Mindfulness

Awakening together

Erik van den Brink

> *The eye you see is not an eye*
> *because you see it;*
> *it is an eye because it sees you.*
>   Antonio Machado
>   (1875–1939)[1]

Those of us who have participated in silent retreats may know the experience of returning home calm and serene, but then, at the first meeting with a family member, friend or colleague, we find ourselves falling back into old familiar, less skilful communication patterns. Disappointed, we realise that we are not as liberated as we had hoped. Apparently, the calmness and insight from individual practice do not automatically extend to encounters with others.

It is certainly plausible that individual mindfulness practice has at least some positive effects on our interpersonal functioning,[2] but the question arises: is there perhaps a more effective way to free ourselves from interpersonal suffering? How would it be if we learned to meditate while we communicate? If we learned to be mindfully present when we speak and listen, could we notice our reactivity more closely and avoid automatically being caught in unhealthy communication patterns? Would this create more space for healthy communication?

Such questions also occupied Gregory Kramer, an American teacher of vipassana or insight meditation, and led him to develop a method called *Insight Dialogue*. A secular training arose from this interpersonal Buddhist practice, which is known as the *Interpersonal Mindfulness Program* (IMP). We will be addressing various aspects of this programme in this chapter: its background, origins, target group, structure and content. We will also discuss the strengths and weaknesses of the programme, as well as practical applications and preliminary research results.

To avoid a dry summary, this chapter is interspersed regularly with texts in italics entitled 'Invitation to the reader', where one can pause for

DOI: 10.4324/9781003262008-3

meditative reflection and gain an experiential taste of the programme. Of course, it must be understood that these individual reflections can never be a substitute for the interpersonal practice under the guidance of a teacher.

Based on Insight Dialogue

In his book *Insight Dialogue: The interpersonal path to freedom* (2007), Gregory Kramer describes how his teachers inspired him with a deep respect for the ancient teachings of the Buddha. The personal and relational aspects of the practice interested him more than the mythical and ritualistic expressions of Buddhism, which are strongly tied to the time and culture in which they arose. He noticed how his insight deepened when his practice focused on the universal human experiences, such as ageing, illness, death and impermanence. After all, these themes had also been the signposts on the path of awakening for Siddhartha Gautama, the later Buddha.

The relational aspect of being human is another universal experience. We are thoroughly social beings, and a lot of suffering is interpersonal suffering. Should then, the path towards liberation from suffering not also be an interpersonal path – at least to a significant extent? The Buddha presumably did not overlook this, but in traditional Buddhist communities, the social aspect was so obvious that it may not have needed explicit mentioning in Buddhist scriptures. However, in today's Western world, we often fail to recognise this, with the result that we tend to put a lot of emphasis on individual practice. It is as if we feel we can only attain insight if we isolate ourselves and refrain from interpersonal contact. Kramer realised that in doing so, we deprive ourselves of an important gateway towards insight, and he sought a way to place the person-to-person encounter right in the midst of it and not outside the practice.

As a student, he became interested in David Bohm (1996) and his approach to dialogue. Bohm was an American-born British quantum physicist and philosopher who worked with the Indian philosopher Krishnamurti. He looked for possibilities for a creative dialogue that is unhindered by our assumptions and prejudices and arises from a participatory consciousness when human beings openly meet. Kramer suspected that such a dialogue could be further deepened through the practice of insight meditation. With his colleague, Terri O'Fallon, he developed a meditative method, *Insight Dialogue Inquiry*, that could be practiced online. Together they researched this method and dedicated their PhD dissertation to it. Kramer then continued his exploration and deepened the method in his meditation groups and as a retreat leader.

Thus, Kramer gradually developed the systematic practice of insight-meditation-in-dialogue, taught from 1995 under the name *Insight Dialogue*. In 2005, a foundation called *Metta Programs* was established, from which Insight Dialogue teachings were offered and where Kramer was assisted by a growing team of teachers trained by him. This evolved into the current *Insight Dialogue Community* which is a community of practitioners dedicated to a Buddhist life path, a *sangha* with both individual and relational practice of insight meditation. The Insight Dialogue teachers and facilitators offer their teachings on a *dana* basis (voluntary contribution). In addition to experiencing Insight Dialogue in retreats, there is the possibility of study and practice in a step-by-step learning path, for which also online meetings are widely used, in smaller or larger groups. The development of meditative and relational qualities and the cultivation of wisdom based on the teachings of the Buddha are central to the practice of Insight Dialogue, which is supported by so-called *guidelines* and *contemplations* (see below).

The birth of the Interpersonal Mindfulness Program (IMP)

Not surprisingly, people were looking for ways to translate Insight Dialogue into a secular context. Many people are not particularly drawn to a Buddhist or spiritual path but wish to learn healthier ways of communicating, seeking proven methods to reduce interpersonal suffering. Indeed, the eight-week Mindfulness-Based Stress Reduction (MBSR) and courses inspired by it, such as Mindfulness-Based Cognitive Therapy (MBCT), have also succeeded in connecting ancient contemplative wisdom with modern science. These mindfulness-based programmes offer a contemporary route to the liberation of suffering, in healthcare and psychology, in education and the workplace. Mindfulness-based programmes help to relate more healthily to stress, painful emotions and difficult thoughts, and to prevent (relapse into) unhealthy behaviour, burn-out or depression. Because so many people suffer from communication stress, it was an obvious step to deepen the stress reduction offered by MBSR with a follow-on training in interpersonal stress reduction. MBSR touches on the theme of communication, but there is insufficient room in the curriculum for a systematic training in mindful communication.

The seeds for the IMP were sown in the first years of this millennium when Kramer invited a group of MBSR trainers to take part in an Insight Dialogue retreat. This was soon followed by initial experiments with pilot courses in interpersonal mindfulness. After several evaluations, this led to the IMP in its current form. Among the pioneers from the MBSR world was Florence Meleo-Meyer, then director of the Oasis Institute for Mindfulness-Based Professional Education and Training, affiliated with the Center for Mindfulness at the University of Massachusetts. She had a special interest in the power of interpersonal practices[3] and was trained by Kramer as an Insight Dialogue teacher. With senior Insight Dialogue and MBSR teacher, Phyllis Hicks, she led the first international IMP teacher trainings. By now, over one hundred IMP trainers have been trained and the programme is offered in the US and several European countries. IMP teachers can only offer the programme when they have gained in-depth experience with Insight Dialogue, have completed the IMP teacher training and have received supervision from a senior IMP teacher.

For whom?

The IMP has been developed as a follow-on training for people who have already completed an MBSR course (or equivalent mindfulness-based programme, such as MBCT). The IMP is for people who are looking for relief from interpersonal stress and wish to cultivate wisdom and compassion in their relationships with others and with themselves. As with other mindfulness courses, a commitment is required to spend between three quarters and one hour daily on home practice. Obviously, the IMP also requires the willingness to participate in interpersonal practices during the sessions, in pairs or small groups, which in other mindfulness-based programmes is usually optional. Prior to starting an IMP course, it is recommended that participants attend an orientation session or meet the teacher individually to assess whether the course is expected to meet their needs.

Although the IMP is designed for participants with diverse backgrounds, the helping professions seem to be particularly attracted by it. This may have to do with the realisation that this programme offers something which has been lacking in their training. Many health professionals, therapists and coaches were trained to work methodically from certain therapeutic or educational models, while time and again it has turned out that the quality of the working relationship is much more important for success than the applied model.[4] There is a need for an accessible, systematic method in developing and deepening interpersonal qualities, which is precisely what interpersonal mindfulness practices offer.[5,6] Qualities such as unconditional positive regard, empathy, compassion, attentive listening and authentic speaking, cannot be learned from books, they can only be cultivated in an actual encounter with other people. Practising meditation-in-dialogue is a particularly effective way of deepening these qualities. When we let the light of our attention shine, not only inwards, but also outwards, in the shared space with the other person, we can awaken together. Each holds a mirror up to the other. When a mirror looks into another mirror, a boundless space emerges that was previously invisible.

The IMP practices are supported by *guidelines* and *contemplations*.

Guidelines

An important pillar of the programme is learning to practise with six guidelines, which come directly from Insight Dialogue and support meditation-in-relationship. Although, for didactic reasons, they are explored separately, they should be viewed as organically interconnected, strengthening each other when practised in combination. In the following box, they are described in the order in which they are introduced in the IMP.

Invitation to the reader

Although the guidelines are intended as support for interpersonal practice, you can become familiar with them in an individual practice. Sit in a comfortable position that supports you in mindful presence. Read the description of the guidelines slowly and let the words sink in. After each guideline, take some time for reflection on the following: what was being touched in you while reading? What are you noticing now? Imagine how this guideline might help you when you are in communication with another person. You may recall previous encounters with others or imagine encounters that may take place in the future.

Pause

The first guideline, Pause, is like a gentle tap on the shoulder inviting us to slow down and stand still in the present moment. What is there to notice right now? Being non-judgementally aware of our experience as it arises, the pleasant and the unpleasant, our likes and dislikes, our tendencies to move towards or move away. Not having to go along with these automatic reactions, but just noticing them. The guideline Pause invites us to step out of our reactivity and to be mindfully present.

Relax

The second guideline, Relax, invites us to embody an attitude of kindness, especially when we experience tension. In the words of Gregory Kramer (2007): 'Relax heals what Pause reveals'. This may sound somewhat strange to those who were taught that mindfulness practices should not be confused with relaxation exercises. Are we not training awareness rather than relaxation? Relaxation can be a pleasant side effect but striving for relaxation only creates more tension. We do not have to tense up, however, when we are invited to relax. What is meant here is to consciously allow relaxation, in body and mind, wherever it can be received: letting a soothing breathing rhythm emerge, surrendering to gravity, feeling the support of the ground or seat that carries us, softening muscles that do not need to be tense – in the face, throat, neck and shoulders, in the chest, abdomen, arms and legs. A relaxed body and a spacious mind go hand in hand. The guideline Relax invites us to soften towards our experience, including difficult thoughts and painful emotions.

Open

The third guideline is Open, inviting us to open our attention from the inside out, like a flower opening towards the light. Our awareness can open to inner sensations in the body. And then expand beyond the boundaries of the body, opening our senses to the outside world, to what we hear and what we see. We can also open towards the shared space with a person we are in communication with, noticing what happens when we look at each other, when our eyes meet, when we hold each other in our gaze. When we open, we open ourselves to giving and receiving, to the mutuality of being in contact with another person.

Attune to Emergence (previously: Trust Emergence[7])

The fourth guideline, Attunement to emergence, invites us to attune to the ever-changing moment, attentively and flexibly. The experience of interpersonal contact is also constantly changing. Trusting ourselves and attuning to the process of comings and goings, with a beginner's mind, an attitude of not-knowing, being in peace with inevitable change and impermanence. As John O'Donohue poetically says: 'like a river flows, carried by the surprise of its own enfolding'.[8]

Listen Deeply

The fifth guideline, Listen Deeply, asks us to be receptive to what the other person is saying and how it is said. We listen not just to the words and their meaning but are receptive with our whole body and our whole being, to the language of sound, tone and rhythm in which the speaker expresses their thoughts and feelings, to the speaker's gaze, face, posture, and gestures. We listen with all our senses, to the other, as well as to what resonates inside us, with sensitivity, sympathy and empathy. Listen deeply is about listening with our hearts.

Speak the Truth

The sixth guideline, Speak the Truth, asks for clarity and discernment in speech. We choose the words that wish to be expressed right now from countless possibilities. This is not about the objective truth. It is about the subjective truth of the moment. We speak from congruence and connectedness with our bodies and emotions, expressing our thoughts and feelings authentically and generously, caring for what we say and how we say it – in words, rhythm and sound, facial expressions and gestures, with respect and kindness for ourselves and for the other person. Speak the truth is about speaking from our hearts.

Contemplations

Another pillar of the programme is practising with contemplations, mindful reflections on various topics that are explored in pairs, or sometimes in threes or fours, with the support of the guidelines. The themes of the contemplations contribute to the cultivation of wisdom while we communicate. Whereas in the original Insight Dialogue the contemplation themes are drawn from traditional Buddhist teachings, in the secular IMP training they are chosen in such a way that they are recognisable and relevant in the daily lives of people with diverse backgrounds. In the first half of the course, contemplation topics link closely to the introduction of particular guidelines. Later in the course, participants increasingly use the support of all guidelines in their contemplations.

Examples of contemplations in the IMP can be found below, in the overview per session.

A brief overview of the programme session by session[9]

The structure of the IMP curriculum is similar to that of MBSR, with eight two-and-a-half-hour sessions, and between the fourth and fifth sessions a full day of practice with six hours of guided practice and lunch. The structure of a typical session is shown in the following box.

A typical session

- Arrival and guided meditation with the teacher recalling guidelines and themes from previous sessions.
- Check-in with the whole group. Participants share what comes up from the home practice of the previous week. In group exchanges, there is usually no round. Sharing in the group is ongoing interpersonal practice, where participants mindfully choose their moment to speak or listen, supported by the guidelines.
- Introduction of the guideline(s) and themes of today's session.
- Interpersonal practice in pairs (sometimes threes or fours), applying one or more guidelines and reflecting on contemplation themes offered by the teacher. The following structure is often used: In the first round person A speaks and person B listens, without having to react verbally. In the second round A and B reverse roles. In the third round, A and B reflect in open dialogue on their experiences in the previous rounds or on what is present right now.
- As required, sitting is alternated with mindful moving or walking or lying down meditation. There may also be a short break for informal practice.
- Sharing of insights from the small group practice with the whole group.
- Home practice for the coming week and handouts. Participants choose a daily formal individual practice (thirty minutes of sitting meditation, body scan, yoga and/or walking meditation), reflect on the session themes, and practise informally with the guidelines in interpersonal contacts.
- Closure with loving kindness meditation towards oneself and others.

An impression of the programme session by session is given below. Although the contemplation topics in the sessions are offered in interpersonal practices, the themes are also very suitable for individual reflection. After all, they are relevant to all of us at any time, also when we are on our own. So any reader wishing to gain an experiential taste of what is being explored is invited to spend some time contemplating what is offered in the 'Invitation to the reader' sections after each session description. *As stated before, this intrapersonal exploration cannot replace the interpersonal practice of a live IMP training.* It can be a valuable individual practice in its own right, however, to mindfully observe what these themes touch in you. So kindly acknowledge your thoughts, feelings and bodily sensations whilst you contemplate the themes. And the guidelines that support us in communication with others may also be very helpful whilst relating to ourselves.

Session 1: Pause – Pleasant and unpleasant experiences

The guideline Pause offers us the possibility to step out of our reactivity in the case of interpersonal stress and mindfully notice our experiences in the present moment, as well as their feeling tone (pleasant, neutral, unpleasant). The feeling tone often triggers automatic reactions if it goes unnoticed. A pleasant feeling tone can attract us, and an unpleasant one repels us. A mindful pause can prevent us from automatically following these tendencies. Participants practise with Pause in pairs, while they contemplate on the feeling tone of experiences, in the body and when meeting others.

Invitation to the reader

Notice what bodily sensations you are experiencing right now and name their feeling tone: is it pleasant, neutral or unpleasant?

Then notice what you see or hear around you. Here also, notice the feeling tone of what you see or hear: is it pleasant, neutral or unpleasant?

Then explore with curiosity one or more unpleasant and pleasant experiences that occurred recently in encounters with others. What was it in that contact that felt pleasant or unpleasant?

Session 2: Relax – Ageing and illness

The guideline Relax offers us the opportunity to allow softening and gentleness when we perceive tension. A lot of tension arises from conditioned tendencies to seek the pleasant and avoid the unpleasant, to focus on differences, compare and judge from our preferences. Can we simply see these conditionings as products of our mind and allow relaxation when they occur? Participants practise in pairs with Pause and Relax whilst they contemplate on ageing and illness. These themes often evoke some tension in most of us, whilst at the same time they are inevitably part of human life and call for kindness.

Invitation to the reader

How does ageing play a role in your life? In yourself? In others?

And how does illness play a role in your life? In yourself? In others?

Session 3: Open – Giving and receiving

When we pause and allow relaxation, we can open our awareness anew to the whole body, to the inner space and beyond the boundaries of the body to the space around us, to what we hear and see. Thus, we can also open to the other person we are in communication with. When our mind is steady and we hold the other person in our gaze, looking them in the eyes, we can open ourselves for giving and receiving. Participants practise in pairs with contemplations around giving and receiving, supported by Pause, Relax and Open.

Invitation to the reader

Reflect on an encounter characterised by genuine generosity. Perhaps you were the giver or receiver, or you witnessed giving and receiving between others. What opened in this giving? What opened in this receiving? What do you notice right now, while you reflect on these experiences of giving and receiving?

Session 4: Attune to Emergence – Change and impermanence

Changeability characterises our experience moment by moment. Grounded in Pause, Relax and Open, we can entrust ourselves and attune to the complexity and instability of our experiences. All experience is impermanent, phenomena arise from what preceded and flow into what follows. It is about attuning to this constantly moving stream of experience, allowing ourselves to be surprised again and again. Participants practise with Attune to Emergence departing from the speaker-listener structure. The open dialogue is ideally suited for attuning to whatever arises, without pre-set agendas. Appropriately, the contemplations are also about change in our lives and resistance to change.

Invitation to the reader

Where and how in your current life are you aware of impermanence and change? Perhaps you are noticing changes in your body? Or in your relationships? In your circumstances? At work?
  And where and how are you noticing resistance to change?

Practice day: Listen Deeply/Speak the Truth – Exploring roles

During the practice day, there are longer periods of silent meditation, as well as guided meditations and interpersonal practices. Formats alternate between sitting, moving, walking and lying down. The last two guidelines are introduced as a pair. Speaking and listening are such complex processes that it is helpful to explore them on different levels. Whilst the speaker practices with Speak the Truth and the listener with Listen Deeply, they contemplate the roles they have in the larger community and in their personal lives. First, they attend to the level of verbal content, and then to the level of the body, emotions and non-verbal communication. After a guided meditation supporting deep relaxation, calmness and clarity, they return to speaking and listening from the deepest level, from their essential being.

Invitation to the reader

What roles do you fulfil in your community, at work and in the society? Which roles do you choose yourself? In which roles do you involuntarily find yourself?

What roles do you fulfil in your intimate relationships, in your family or circle of close friends? Which roles do you take on yourself? In which roles do you involuntarily find yourself?

Who are you beyond all these roles? Who are you in essence?

Session 5: Interpersonal 'hungers'

Now that all six guidelines have been addressed in previous sessions, they can be jointly supportive, in various combinations, in the contemplations that follow. The theme of the fifth session is interpersonal 'hungers' (desires, needs).[10] When we are governed by these hungers unnoticed and they are driving our interpersonal behaviour, they can be a source of deep suffering, for ourselves as well as for others. In the contemplations participants explore three interpersonal desires or needs in pairs, supported by all the guidelines. Each can also show up as its negative, as aversion to or fear of the contrary.

Invitation to the reader

How does the desire for pleasure (or avoidance of pain) manifest itself in contact with others in your life? What do you do to experience pleasure and connection? What do you do to avoid pain and loneliness?

How does the desire to be seen by others (or the fear of not being seen) manifest itself in your relationships?

How does the desire for invisibility (or the fear of being seen) manifest itself in your relationships?

Session 6: Limiting habits

In the sixth session, participants explore what can get in the way of communication. In Buddhism five hindrances are mentioned that often surface in meditation: 1. Wanting and craving, 2. Aversion and ill will, 3.

Restlessness and worry, 4. Dullness and inattention, and 5. Doubt. These hindrances are referred to as 'thieves of the heart' or 'limiting habits' and can be equally challenging in interpersonal practice. It is important to realise that hindrances are an inevitable part of the practice. When we examine them, mindfully and gently, they can greatly contribute to the awakening of insight and compassion. Participants practise with Listen Deeply and Speak the Truth in a similar 'layered' way as during the practice day, whilst they contemplate on some of these limiting habits that can separate us from others.

Invitation to the reader

Reflect on recent encounters with others where one or more of the limiting habits stood in the way. Consider, for example, an encounter where aversion and anger were prominent, in yourself or in the other person. What about restlessness and worry (ruminating about the past or the future)? Or doubt?

Session 7: Remembering and cultivating the good

In the seventh session, the contemplation theme is 'remembering and cultivating wholesome qualities'. This theme is supported by positive psychology and neuroscientific findings. Healthy behaviours become increasingly anchored in our neural networks when we cultivate them through practice. This time, participants practise in threes, with one speaker and two listeners, whilst they let themselves be supported by the guidelines. The listeners offer a receptive field to the speaker, who is invited to generously share what they experience as beneficial in their lives. The listeners then reflect one by one on what touched them in a wholesome way, whilst they received what the speaker shared. Finally, the speaker reflects on the listeners' feedback.

Invitation to the reader

Where and how do beneficial thoughts, words and deeds manifest in your life? Perhaps you spend time practising meditation, caring for the well-being of yourself and others. Maybe you do beneficial work for those in need, for animals, nature, the planet. Let yourself be touched by what comes to mind.

Session 8: Review and ending

In the last session participants look back on the course in threes or fours. There is no special structure now, and they let themselves be supported by all guidelines. The contemplation is on what they have learned, what has changed during the course and what changes they wish for the future. This is followed by a plenary evaluation and exploration of how to continue with practising individually and interpersonally. The course concludes with a loving-kindness meditation.

Invitation to the reader

What have you learned from reading about the IMP course and from having an experiential taste of the guidelines and contemplations? Have you noticed any changes?

While you reflect, allow the support of Pause, Relax, Open and Attune to emergence. What beneficial changes do you wish for yourself in the future? Listen attentively to your deeper needs. Perhaps you can let one or more kind wishes or phrases come up and let them flow through you, letting the words arise from the generosity of your heart – Speak the truth, also to yourself. Noticing how the words are received – Listen deeply, also to yourself.

Strengths of the programme

The IMP offers a clear structure and the sessions build on each other to create a cohesive fabric. It is didactically powerful to introduce the guidelines one by one and to link them to corresponding contemplations. The six guidelines offer simplicity and support in the complex reality of communication, offering a space in which wisdom and compassion can awaken in the presence of another person. The guidelines become increasingly deeply anchored from the guided practices in the sessions and also from following the assignments for home practice. It is an advantage that the programme has been designed as a follow-on course and participants already have experience with mindfulness practices, training in a group and relating mindfully to stressful experiences. This allows for more calmness and stability of mind when facing the challenges of interpersonal practices. The similar structure and content of the IMP to the foundational mindfulness-based programmes is another strength and the individual and interpersonal practices strongly reinforce each other. The guidelines are also helpful in individual practice where we meet the challenges in relating to ourselves.

A gradual exposure to challenging experiences is further supported by practising in turn as speaker and as listener. This division of roles offers more calm, space and concentration to observe reactivity emerge and apply the guidelines accordingly. A randomly composed group offers the advantage of first practising with people one does not know so well. After all, communication patterns are often firmly established and operate automatically with people we share longer histories with. With a fellow practitioner who is less familiar, there is more room to notice reactivity as soon as it manifests itself and respond mindfully.

Applications

The IMP has a broad applicability in diverse settings. The course appeals to graduates of foundational mindfulness programmes in the general public. The impression is that most IMP teachers offer the course in open settings or primary care, to relatively healthy, self-referring participants. To my knowledge, the programme has not yet been offered to mental health clients, and caution seems advisable in this group. The course may be less suitable or even destabilising for vulnerable people with high levels of social anxiety, relational problems and psychiatric histories, which may require considerable adaptations and even more gradual exposure.

During the COVID-19 pandemic, many teachers have been offering courses online. This differs from meeting physically, but with the necessary adaptations and ample use of break-out rooms, the IMP can be satisfactorily taught online. Following the IMP as an intensive training of three or more days in a retreat setting is another worthwhile alternative for those who have difficulty accessing an eight-week course. Some mindfulness training institutes include this format in their continuing education programmes.

The IMP appears to be a valuable training for mindfulness teachers themselves and this is another field of application. Mindfulness teachers who followed the IMP often report back how the interpersonal practice enhances their teaching skills and deepens the mindful dialogue and inquiry with their participants. The interpersonal mindfulness practices are also easily integrated into teacher training courses and enrich other mindfulness-based programmes, for instance, Mindfulness-Based Compassionate Living (MBCL). MBCL is – like the IMP – a follow-on course that Frits Koster and I developed in 2007.[11] We have used the ID guidelines and the speaker-listener structure in our teachings and found that the programmes deepen each other. Those who have experience with both MBCL and the IMP notice how the compassion practice helps them in their interpersonal practice and vice versa.

An important application is to offer the IMP to healthcare workers, therapists, counsellors, and coaches – in fact to anyone who works with people. Many in the helping professions are vulnerable to burnout, a decline in empathy and failing communication, and there is mounting evidence that they can benefit from mindfulness-based programmes.[12] It is to be expected that the IMP will be increasingly introduced in this field. For instance, Frits and I have offered the eight-week IMP successfully to mental health professionals at the centre where we worked in the Netherlands, which was also subject to research (see below). I also regularly offer a much-appreciated IMP intensive format to doctors and medical coaches in Belgium.

Finally, another interesting application field is to adapt the IMP for leadership development. A British group is currently working on this.[13]

First research results

Empirical research of the IMP is still at a very early stage. At the Centre for Integrative Psychiatry in Groningen, the Netherlands, an initial feasibility study of the programme was carried out among mental healthcare workers, including doctors, nurses, psychologists and other therapists.[14] The results of 25 participants in two consecutive training courses were compared with a control group of 22. The programme showed good feasibility and there were no dropouts. The qualitative evaluation showed great satisfaction with the content and format of the programme and the trainers. The relevance for their own profession was considered as high. Some adverse effects were reported such as excessive self-consciousness and flashbacks/dreams. Some mentioned the strong Buddhist feel in some of the themes ('hungers', 'hindrances', 'impermanence'). Quantitative results showed a significant increase in self-compassion and empathy, and a significant decrease in compassion fatigue and reactivity to inner experiences. No valid scale was available for compassion for others. The scales that were used predated the discussion around compassion fatigue. Empathy distress fatigue has been proposed as a more accurate concept.[15]

Clearly, more research into IMP is necessary, with larger numbers, clear definitions, adequate measuring instruments and both quantitative and qualitative analyses.

Limitations of the programme

The standard IMP curriculum does not prescribe the use of audio material. Many participants appreciate being able to listen to guided meditations with introductions to guidelines and/or contemplations to support their home practice. After all, audio aids are also common in other mindfulness-based programmes. Some trainers resolve this by recording guided meditations during sessions or offer previously recorded audio files. The IMP handouts are also rather sparse. Many participants appreciate more supporting information, particularly because there is little accessible IMP literature available yet.

A serious limitation, in my opinion, is that although the programme aims to be secular, it has a stronger Buddhist atmosphere than most other mindfulness programmes. The influence of the Insight Dialogue Community with Gregory Kramer as its founder is relatively large compared to the secular influences. Possibly this is also a reason why until now there has been little academic interest in the IMP and the research into it has been scarce. In 2017, an influential consensus article appeared on the criteria which a mindfulness-based programme should meet to be recognised as such. The first essential characteristic is that the programme 'is informed by theories and practices that draw from a confluence of contemplative traditions, science, and the major disciplines of medicine, psychology and education'.[16] In its present form, the IMP appears to be a confluence of a broad, dominant Insight Dialogue river with a few tiny streams from science and non-religious disciplines. A more balanced influx from secular disciplines would benefit the further development, acceptance and dissemination of the IMP.

Conclusion

The IMP has great potential to alleviate and prevent interpersonal suffering. In today's digital age, which offers us so many temptations to engage in superficial communications through social media, and with so many people feeling lonely and disconnected, the IMP meets the universal human need for genuine connection and social intimacy. It is a suitable programme for people who have already followed a foundational mindfulness course and wish to practise meditation-in-dialogue. It draws on the strength and simplicity of the Insight Dialogue guidelines and works with contemplative topics that touch every human being. It has a wide applicability in the personal and professional lives of many people. Experiences of mindfulness trainers and health professionals with the IMP are very positive, and initial research results are encouraging. The interpersonal practice forms of the IMP can be easily integrated into other mindfulness-based programmes and training courses for professionals. More input from science, healthcare, psychology and education could give the programme a more solid basis.

Finally

I wrote this chapter with a mixture of joy and trepidation. Clearly, I am happy to contribute to greater awareness of this valuable programme and at the same time I realise that a concise description can never do it justice. There is no substitute for an IMP live experience in a group with a recognised IMP teacher. I sincerely hope that this chapter inspires readers to participate in an eight-week IMP course or an intensive IMP training, or in an Insight Dialogue retreat or meditation group. I am deeply grateful to Gregory Kramer and his work, the Insight Dialogue Community and the developers of the IMP, with special thanks to Florence Meleo-Meyer and Phyllis Hicks for their valuable comments on an earlier draft of this chapter (Table 3.1).

Table 3.1 Resources

RESOURCES

Books:

- Gregory Kramer (2007). *Insight Dialogue: The interpersonal path to freedom.* Boston, MA: Shambhala.
- Florence Meleo-Meyer (2016). Interpersonal practices: A transformational force in the MBIs. In: D. McCown, D.K. Reibel, & M.S. Micozzi (Eds.), *Resources for teaching mindfulness – An international handbook* (pp. 69–91). Switzerland: Springer International.

Website:

- www.insightdialogue.org – website of the *Insight Dialogue Community*, with a special page on the IMP: www.insightdialogue.org/interpersonal-mindfulness-program.

Let me hear you

Let me hear you.
Speak your heart
and empty out those dark corners.

Words unspoken
cannot bring joy.
Let them dance,
even if their steps first falter.

Trust that what emerges
will be warmed by the sun,
will be sheltered from the wind
by my listening.

Let words that have been furled
tighter and tighter inside
emerge and stretch and sway.
Watch them lighten

and feel your heart lift
as their weight eases
and they flow out in the world
like butterflies, to land or float away.

Let them go
and see your soul dance
to sweet silence
in the hallowed space that remains.

Rachel Holstead[17]

Notes

1   Machado, A. (1924). Freely translated from: 'Proverbios y cantares' in *Nuevas canciones*. Madrid: Mundo Latino.
2   Parker, S.C., Nelson, B.W., Epel, E.S., & Siegel, D.J. (2015). The science of presence – A central mediator of the interpersonal benefits of mindfulness. In: K.W. Brown, J.D. Creswell & R.M. Ryan (Eds.), *Handbook of mindfulness – Theory, research, and practice* (pp. 225–244). New York, NY: The Guilford Press.
3   Meleo-Meyer, F. (2016). Interpersonal practices: A transformational force in the MBIs. In: D. McCown, D. K. Reibel & M. S. Micozzi (Eds.), *Resources for teaching mindfulness – An international handbook* (pp. 69–91). Switzerland: Springer International.
4   Wampold, B.E., & Imel, Z.E. (2015). *The great psychotherapy debate: The evidence for what makes psychotherapy work* (2nd ed.). London: Routledge.
5   Kramer, G., Meleo-Meyer, F., & Lee Turner, M. (2008). Cultivating mindfulness in relationship: Insight dialogue and the interpersonal mindfulness program. In: S.F. Hick & T. Bien (Eds.), *Mindfulness and the therapeutic relationship* (pp. 195–214). New York, NY: The Guilford Press.
6   Surrey J.L., & Kramer, G. (2013). Relational mindfulness. In: C.K. Germer, R.D. Siegel, & P.R. Fulton (Eds.), *Mindfulness and psychotherapy* (pp. 94–111). New York, NY: The Guilford Press.
7   For two decades *Trust Emergence* was used to refer to this guideline. Because it was frequently misunderstood – as if one should trust everything that arises – Kramer decided in 2018 to change the wording to *Attune to Emergence*. Source: www.gregorykramer.org/new-guideline-wording-attune-to-emergence/, accessed 14th January 2022.
8   O'Donohue, J. (2000). From 'Fluid' in *Conamara Blues*. London: Bantam Books.
9   This overview is based on the generally available resources mentioned above and on the IMP workbook I compiled with Frits Koster, which we only share with participants in our IMP courses. The full IMP manual is solely accessible to those who followed an IMP teacher training and can be found in: Kramer, G., Hicks, P. K., & Meleo-Meyer, F. (2019), *Interpersonal mindfulness program: A teachers outline & resource guide*, Seattle: Metta Programs.
10   The use of the word 'hungers' may seem somewhat strange for those who are unfamiliar with Buddhist teachings, where being caught in 'hunger', 'craving' and 'attachment' is seen as a major cause of suffering. In a secular setting we can speak of 'desires' or 'needs' instead, which are more accessible.
11   Van den Brink, E. & Koster, F. (2015). *Mindfulness-Based Compassionate Living – A new training programme to deepen mindfulness with heartfulness*. London: Routledge.
12   Lomas, T., Medina, J.C., Ivtzan, I., Rupprecht, S., Hart, R., & Eiroa-Orosa, F.J. (2017). A systematic review of the impact of mindfulness on the well-being of healthcare professionals. *Journal of Clinical Psychology, 74*(3), 319–355.
13   Donaldson-Feilder, E., Lewis, R., Yarker, J., & Whiley, L.A. (December 2021). Interpersonal mindfulness in leadership development: A Delphi Study. *Journal of Management Education*. doi: 10.1177/10525629211067183.
14   Bartels-Velthuis, A.A., Van den Brink, E., Koster, F., & Hoenders. H.J.R. (2020). The interpersonal mindfulness program for health care professionals: A feasibility study. *Mindfulness, 11*, 2629–2638.

15 Klimecki, O., & Singer, T. (2011). Empathic distress fatigue rather than com-
    passion fatigue? Integrating findings from empathy research in psychology
    and social neuroscience. In: B. Oakley, A. Knafo, G. Madhavan, & D.S.
    Wilson (Eds.), *Pathological altruism* (pp. 368–383). Oxford University Press.
16 Crane, R.S., Brewer, J., Feldman, C., Kabat-Zinn, J. Santorelli S., Williams,
    J.M.G., & Kuyken, W. (2017). What defines mindfulness-based programs? The
    warp and the weft. *Psychological Medicine, 47,* 990–999.
17 Reproduced with kind permission from www.rachelholstead.net/these-
    are-not-my-words. (accessed in July 2022).

Chapter 4

Green Zone Communication

Our day-to-day conversations as mindfulness practice

Gregory Heffron, Esther Hasselman and Chris Trani

> *Every human life is a work of art.*
> Susan Gillis-Chapman

How did Green Zone Communication evolve?

Green Zone Communication is an approach for mindful communication developed by author and senior Buddhist teacher Susan Gillis Chapman. Chapman is a retired psychologist and relationship/family therapist with more than 50 years of experience of mindfulness and meditation. In 2009, she began working with Gregory Heffron, senior trainer and Executive Director of Green Light Communication. Gillis Chapman and Heffron were both trained in mindfulness in the Shambhala Buddhist organisation, founded in 1970 by the Tibetan teacher Chögyam Trungpa Rinpoche. Esther Hasselman and Chris Trani are both trainers with years of experience who became teachers of Green Zone Communication in 2020.

In 2012, after 12 years of testing concepts and practices with many groups, Chapman published a guide to her approach: *The five keys to mindful communication.*

Chapman and Heffron also provide workshops and retreats – both live and online – to students in countries as diverse as the UK, the Netherlands, Switzerland, Chile, Poland, Ukraine, Belgium, Canada and the US. In recent years, they've trained advanced students in North America and Europe to become Green Zone group Leaders and Teachers. Green Zone groups borrow the term used in war zones. Traditionally, these were safe havens where soldiers did not fight and could set down their weapons and regain their sense of humanity. (We'll come back later to the term 'green zone'.)

Who can benefit?

The method is suitable for both beginners and more experienced mindfulness practitioners. Many people today study mindfulness, and some go further to deeply study teachings on compassion. Mindful communication

DOI: 10.4324/9781003262008-4

training is a natural outcome of this exploration, and the advanced Green Zone Communication workshops are filled with those who want to take mindfulness and compassion beyond the abstract and into a living practice to provide immediate relief for themselves and others.

That said, a green zone is a safe place for learning and discovery, and even people without any experience of mindfulness can make giant leaps with this method. Green Zone Communication is particularly enriching for caregivers, teachers and trainers, who can gain valuable new perspectives that they can apply in their professional practice.

What is Green Zone Communication?

We all experience misunderstandings and discomfort in our daily conversations. Sometimes they're so minor we hardly notice. Other times, they shake the foundations of our lives. Green Zone Communication offers many practical tools to discover where the problems lie and how to adapt our communication – both within ourselves and between ourselves and others – to determine whether communication can go forward, what kind of communication is appropriate and where we as individuals exist in relation to our conversation partner(s).

Green Zone Communication focuses on our everyday conversations and activities through incorporating the principles of our individual mindfulness practice into our interactions with others. Sometimes in conversations, we are present and connected. But oftentimes our attention flickers elsewhere. Green Zone Communication helps us to listen and communicate more deeply, aided by the following simple models and rules of thumb.

Considering everyone as healthy and whole

The foundation of Green Zone Communication comes from Contemplative Psychology, pioneered by Chogyam Trungpa in the early 1970s, and taught first at Naropa University. In contrast to many forms of psychology, in which the focus is more on pathology, in Contemplative Psychology, we are all seen as fundamentally whole and healthy – no matter how confused we might be from day to day.

This is not just a nice idea. When we practise mindfulness, we can experience this directly. We consciously bring our attention back to the direct, sensory experience in the moment, and we can feel that what we encounter as living beings is complete and good at a basic sensory level. In other words, there is nothing wrong with the pure, direct experience of sitting on a chair, or the texture of the book we are holding in our hands.

Most of the time, however, it doesn't stop there. Very quickly, our habitual patterns rear their heads and mental constructions emerge in which something feels 'off'. If the chair feels hard or our hands feel dry, we quickly judge this to be a problem. Emotions, thoughts and physical feelings then arise in response to this judgement.

In the practice of mindfulness, we notice these reactions and we are able to peel back the experience to the moment of the first, pure experience, in which nothing is wrong and in which we are complete and healthy. Here, we can distinguish if there is an actual problem that needs to be addressed, or whether our mind is just craving distraction and creating unnecessary drama. In either situation, our direct experience of pleasure or discomfort is seen as healthy and without problem.

In the example of having dry hands, the artificial drama ('If I don't get the lotion right now, I won't be able to function!') does not have to be seen as a problem. Instead, it is viewed – honestly – as creating artificial/ optional pain. The dry skin is just a fact. The exaggerated drama is that we cannot experience this without feeling – even in a small way – that 'life is bad'. Of course, the sensation of dry skin isn't pleasant. But in many cases, this kind of exaggeration isn't alerting us to a real-life crisis. Instead, we've unconsciously made a reasonable and tolerable experience into a 'bad' experience.

> *Meditation tunes us into the flow of our natural communication system.*
> *(...) This communication system operates at the most fundamental level of*
> *our awareness, where we accommodate the first moment of an experience.*
> Susan Gillis Chapman

Our natural communication system

Green Zone Communication describes our natural communication system as 'an awake body, a tender heart, and an open mind':

- Our awake body is in contact with the direct sensory experiences in the moment.
- Our tender heart is in contact with our feelings, compassion and empathy.
- Our open mind is open to what unfolds in the moment through ongoing curiosity.

These three aspects of our natural communication system are connected, and they complement each other. If we are in touch with all three aspects, communication can flow freely. When this is the case, we are complete and healthy, free from habitual patterns and mental constructs. Here, even intense communication can be powerful, vibrant and genuine.

However, if we become out of touch with one of these aspects, our mental constructs take over. With a closed heart, we become harsh. In Green Zone Communication we call this a 'Heartless Mind'. Another pattern is called

'Mindless Heart', in which we close our mind and let our emotions take over. We will say more about these two patterns later on.

One effective way we can restore contact with our body, heart and mind is with mindfulness meditation. See the audio exercise 'Getting in touch with our natural communication system'.

Integrating mindfulness into our conversations

Green Zone Communication is an active form of mindfulness where our focus shifts from being a solo practice of sitting in stillness and silence to the activity of daily life, specifically, our daily conversations with others. Just as in our usual mindfulness exercises, in Green Zone conversations we bring our attention back to the present moment. We notice thoughts, emotions and physical sensations without needing to interfere with them. We are present in the moment with friendly, open attention and perceive our experiences exactly as they are.

In a conversation, however, we are receiving much more sensory input than when we practise individually, such as the content of the conversation and the voice and facial expressions of our conversation partner. In Green Zone Communication, we practise noticing all of these experiences purely and directly, without giving in to the mindless or compulsive reactions and responses that arise. As in individual meditation, in conversations we move back and forth between open attention and closed reactions.

We are all connected to each other, and we influence each other in every contact, even if we are not aware of it. The Vietnamese monk Thich Nhat Hanh calls this *interbeing*. If we take time for the conversation, if we are fully present and prepared to listen to the other person without preconceived ideas about the outcome, then we feel this connection, this feeling of 'We First' (or 'We Together'). Energy flows between everyone in the conversation, there is an open exchange and co-creation takes place. The whole is more than the sum of its parts.

Sooner or later, something will happen in a conversation that makes one or both of the conversation partners feel disconnected. The energy no longer flows. We hear the word 'cinnamon' and our attention is suddenly focused on our dear grandmother's apple pie, and no longer on the personal story our friend is telling us. Or we see a frown on the face of the person we're talking to and get lost in a frenzy of thoughts about what we may have done wrong. Suddenly, we find ourselves on our own little island, telling ourselves imaginary stories about ourselves and others. We disappear into mental constructs, which do not originate from the experience in the moment. Instead, these arise from our emotional patterns that were created in the past, often by painful experiences that triggered anxiety. This can lead us to a sense of self-absorption and separateness, where

Figure 4.1 'Me First' and 'We Together'.

© *Esther Hasselman*

we feel forced to make a choice between our own needs and the needs of someone else.

As soon as our attention is brought back into the here-and-now, free from stories and ideas, we are again open and connected with the other person. There is enough space for everyone's needs to be acknowledged. This opening can happen because of an unexpected sensory experience, or because our conversation partner wakes us up with an unexpected remark. During conversations, we constantly move back and forth between 'Me First' and 'We Together'.

Opening and closing: the traffic light model

The 'We Together' mode is more empowering and more effective than the 'Me First' mode. 'We Together' is the foundation of our natural communication system. Although we aspire to remain in this open state during conversations, it is not uncommon for us to open and close many times. It is a dynamic, ever-changing process. This is perfectly normal, and Green Zone Communication does not aim to prevent us from closing down and retreating into 'Me First'. Instead, we aim to learn how to navigate this process in real-time, and to find ways to reconnect with our natural communication system of awake body, tender heart and open mind.

The process of opening and closing is represented in Green Zone Communication by a traffic light: green is open and red is closed. The third light, yellow, represents an intermediate or transitional phase.

Green: traffic flows

The green light refers to the flow of open experiences from moment to moment, in contact with ourselves and our surroundings, with an innate awareness and intention of 'We Together'. It also refers to the first, unprocessed experience in the moment, free from habitual patterns and mental constructions. We are healthy, clear and openly present with what unfolds in the moment. Our natural communication system is active.

When the light is green, there is a friendly connection in the present moment, and we have the best interests of ourselves and others at heart. This creates a foundation in which communication flows back and forth. We can discuss anything with each other – even if we don't agree with each other, or if we have a difficult message to deliver.

Red: traffic has stopped

But then, something can happen that causes us to close down and create barriers between ourselves and the other person. This stops the conversation from flowing. The red light refers to this experience.

When we are in a closed-off state, there is no longer 'We Together'. We have erected virtual walls around ourselves, and our intention is now 'Me First'. We are not really in contact with each other, and at least one of us is no longer listening fully to the other person. This happens unconsciously. But usually, after a while, we notice that we have been closed and that communication was no longer flowing. For example, we notice that we were behaving in ways that were defensive, dominant, pushy, demeaning or clingy. As soon as we notice this, we automatically move from red to yellow (or, more rarely, directly to green).

It is perfectly normal and human to go back and forth between open and closed communication, between the green and red lights. We do not need to criticise ourselves for this. In fact, if we allow and explore these experiences, we can get to know ourselves better and grow in being consciously and attentively present in our conversations. So when we notice the red light, we can simply pause for a moment and be compassionate with ourselves and others – remembering our common humanity, and recognizing that the red light is not bad, it's just a painful part of being human.

Yellow: traffic is changing

The yellow traffic light represents an intermediate stage, the transition from green to red or – as we literally see it in some countries – from red to green. We often miss the yellow light when it flashes. Or, as we may do when driving in traffic, we may notice it but try to rush through. In Green Zone Communication, we appreciate the yellow light as an important part of communication that both informs us and potentially empowers us if we can learn to slow down and pay attention.

The yellow light is characterised by disorientation and doubt. We do not understand what has happened, and we are looking for clarity. There are fragments of possible explanations, which are not directly based on the current situation, but more on memories and imagination. Uncertainty sets in; we wonder if we have done something wrong, immediately followed by self-doubt and fear that there is something fundamentally wrong with us.

Chapman distinguishes five categories of fears that come into play when the light is yellow:[1]

1. The fear of being unwelcome.
2. The fear of being worthless.
3. The fear of being unforgivable.
4. The fear of being unlovable.
5. The fear of being inadequate and powerless.

This fragile yellow light, with its fears and self-doubt, can also be recognised as shame. We have nothing to grip, no certainty and no clarity. This feels groundless and unbearable, and there is a strong reflex to close ourselves off completely and flee into the red light. We usually do this by turning the fear we feel outwards, in our projections onto others.

For example, while in the yellow light we are afraid of not being welcome, in the 'red light mode' we project this outwards and make the other person feel unwelcome by tuning them out of our awareness. Our fear of being worthless expresses itself as contempt for the other person, and so on.

Yet there is hope when the light is yellow. In contrast to the closed, frozen red light, the yellow light is not yet completely closed and there is room to explore what is happening. If we acknowledge the vulnerability of the yellow light, we can protect and support its tenderness. Here, we can offer ourselves and/or the other person a *green zone*: a safe place in which we are given space and are invited to explore the tenderness with curiosity, as a way to return to the green light. See page 62 for how to create a green zone.

Example: the thoughts and feelings exercise

In the eight-week mindfulness training (MBCT and MBSR), the exercise 'Thoughts and Feelings' is done, in which participants are invited to imagine the following:

Exercise: Thoughts and Feelings

You are walking down the street and on the other side of the street you see someone you know. You smile and wave at that person, but he or she just continues walking. What comes to mind?

After this short scenario, participants list their reactions, making a distinction between physical sensations, emotions and thoughts. It turns out that the participants all have different interpretations of the event, partly based on previous experiences. Some people have a positive or neutral experience, but the majority interpret the lack of response to the greeting as negative.

Let's look at the reactions from the 'Thoughts and Feelings Exercise' in the light of the traffic light model. If we notice that the other person is not responding, we may travel through the three colours:

1. *Green.* The first reaction in the moment is often one of surprise: 'What is going on?' This is the moment when we are open, healthy and connected: the light is green, our natural communication system is active.
2. *Yellow.* In a split second, we look for an explanation to clear up our uncertainty. For many people, this uncertainty translates into insecurity about ourselves. We unconsciously ask ourselves what we have done wrong, causing the light to turn yellow. We feel unsettled and wonder what could be wrong with us. Maybe we are unforgivable, or unlovable. Maybe we are 'totally worthless'. The scenarios that flash by trigger fear and uncertainty. We experience this 'yellow light' phase as unbearable.
3. *Red.* We unconsciously choose a way out of our self-doubt. We turn the arrows that were initially directed inwards outwards, and project them on other people. This allows us to avoid feeling insecure about ourselves. Suddenly we have a story about the other person that explains why he or she has not returned our greetings. Now the *other* person – in our red-light view – has become unforgivable, unlovable or worthless. We are so eager to get rid of our discomfort about ourselves that we create stories in our heads that justify these judgements. For example, we might think: 'He has obviously never been trustworthy', or 'What a naive and stupid person', or 'I don't matter to him. Just wait until he needs me one day'. Whatever our red light reaction, we are completely separated from the full humanity of the other person and from our real experience in the present moment – such as disappointment, sadness or surprise. Instead, we become absorbed in our mental constructions, which Chapman calls 'toxic certainty'.

We usually go through these stages unconsciously – all of a sudden, the light is red and we don't know how it happened. The good news is that we can reflect and look more deeply at our reaction to the events, gaining insight into our triggers and mental constructs. Because this means consciously examining our yellow light fears, such a tender and delicate 'peeling away' process requires a safe environment – a green zone.

Creating green zones

A green zone is a safe place where we are present and connected with ourselves, our environment and others. When we feel safe, there is no need to manage the situation with stories or to protect ourselves. As mentioned earlier, the term 'green zone' refers to a safe haven within a war zone. A green zone can be any place or setting that evokes a feeling of safety and connectedness in the here and now. Some people experience nature as a green zone. Some people experience certain places in their homes or spaces in their community as a green zone (e.g. our backyard garden, a concert, or an art museum). In a green zone, we can open up and have a genuine and powerful conversation – even just with ourselves.

Green Zone Communication always starts with ourselves, with the invitation to experience and trust the open connectedness of our own natural communication system. This is our own *intra*personal green zone, where we can welcome all our experiences – green, yellow and red – examine them and ultimately, with the power of attention, transform them into further insight, confidence and appreciation. Open, connected listening to ourselves happens, for example, during a walk in nature, or during meditation – our personal green zone.

We can take this greater self-understanding into an *inter*personal green zone – called a 'social green zone' – which we share with one or more green zone friends. Together, we can create a space in which to listen and communicate, and which invites and encourages openness. The guidelines of the traffic light are important here:

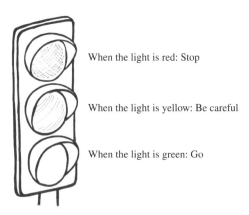

When the light is red: Stop

When the light is yellow: Be careful

When the light is green: Go

Figure 4.2 The guidelines of the traffic light model.

© *Esther Hasselman*

When the light is green: Go

The conversation flows, and we only need to monitor lightly whether the light is still green. We are willing to ask ourselves whether we are still mindfully present in the moment, whether we are open and connected with an intention of 'We Together' and whether we have an agenda that could get in the way of an open conversation.

Green light means that we stay attentive to what's happening in the conversation and are willing to change course and flow in a different direction in response to what is happening in the present moment. This does not mean that difficult subjects cannot be discussed or that differing or even opposing opinions cannot be expressed. Quite the contrary. What it means is that we are thoughtful about how we enter into these discussions. The green light awareness knows to check in beforehand whether this is the right moment for it, whether it still makes sense and whether we can move forward while staying connected – both with the other person and also with our own truth.

When the light is red: Stop

The red light is self-perpetuating, feeding on itself and triggering more yellow and red light reactions in others. We can easily end up in a vicious circle of isolation, blaming, clinging and so on. Therefore, in order not to fight fire with fire, it's important to learn to deal with the red light in a gentle and compassionate way.

Even when we have been isolated in a red light state and absorbed in mental constructions, sooner or later something happens that makes it possible for our light to go green again. We call this a *positive interruption* (a topic we'll come back to soon).

The path from red to green almost always runs through the yellow light. We acknowledge that there is something vulnerable behind the red light, and we want to invite and encourage that.

When the light is yellow: Be careful

This suggests that we protect and support the tenderness of the yellow light. It invites us to stay present in the yellow light and explore it further. That way, we can transform the yellow light and reconnect with the green. If we can make the choice to engage with the yellow, the insights we find can be the source of real empowerment. This alone can change our communication and relationships for the better. But it is easier said than done.

The yellow light is one of the most vulnerable and yet powerful parts of Green Zone Communication, yet it can easily escape our attention. Why? We typically flee straight away into the red light as if the yellow light was never even there. We ignore the yellow light because it feels like it's dissolving our sense of security.

Right at these moments, we can choose to allow ourselves to enter into a green zone. Here, we have access to gentle, protective, compassionate support to learn how to stay present with and attend to the intensity of our yellow light.

Two specific red light patterns

The traffic light is not static: the colour is constantly changing. One moment the light is red, the next it is green. This is a dynamic and entirely subjective process, perceived by each of us through our own filters, insights and intuition. We're not trying to compare our experience with some abstract 'objective reality' – which isn't available to us mere mortals. Instead, this approach asks us to tune into what we can actually perceive, understanding that we will of course have human limitations and red-light biases. Our awake body, tender heart and open mind will have to encounter and sort through these biases over time. But in the meanwhile, we can get started right now, right where we are.

This is not abstract, we can experience this in real-time. While we are having a conversation with someone, it may be that at some point we feel open (green), while we experience the state of our conversation partner as closed (red). The next moment, the red of the other person may trigger a reaction in us, causing us to move towards yellow or red ourselves. Or the other person moves consciously or unconsciously to yellow or green, in response to our open, green state. It is an ongoing process of change that is always happening, whether we are aware of it or not.

As we saw in the Thoughts and Feelings Exercise, people react differently to events in their lives. When we fall into the red light, some of us lose contact mainly with the heart ('Heartless Mind'), while others lose contact mainly with the head ('Mindless Heart'). In relationships, these two red light patterns work out very differently. 'Mindless Heart' is a dysfunctional way of connecting, and 'Heartless Mind' is a dysfunctional way of distancing ourselves from each other.

'Heartless Mind': when love turns to hate

'Heartless Mind' uses logic to justify harming others

No matter how hard we try, sooner or later something will happen in our lives or in our daily conversations that will cause us pain, friction or conflict. This is simply part of being human, but we may find it difficult to face. Instead of being mindfully aware of the negative experience, we easily dismiss it. If we do not want to feel pain, we close ourselves off from the signals of our heart. And we end up in a state called 'Heartless Mind'. Our mind then forms a strategy to justify that we have suppressed our empathy and compassion. We build a red zone – an unsafe environment in which we view the world with closed, fearful and hostile 'Me First' intentions. The 'Heartless Mind' pattern can quickly escalate into arguments, bullying and even war.

The 'Heartless Mind' pattern builds from green through yellow to red, after which it can escalate further in four stages, according to Chapman. It begins with an experience of pain or discomfort, a normal human experience. There is nothing wrong with this in itself, and in this unprocessed, pure experience of the moment, the light is still green. However, it can soon change to yellow if we become afraid of the experience of pain. The pain evokes feelings of vulnerability and insecurity, and this triggers a red light strategy to avoid the pain. A toxic certainty arises that this experience of pain 'should not be happening'. This *complaint* is the first phase of a 'Heartless Mind' pattern. Instead of feeling compassion for our pain, we try to move away from it and get rid of it, which brings us to the second phase: *divisiveness*. We look for someone (or a group) whom we can blame for the pain. The hidden agenda is that pain is a sign that we need to be punished. But we don't want to be punished, and our strategy is to find someone else to punish. We use objectifying, devaluing language so that our target no longer appears to be a flesh and blood human being, but a target that we now – in the third phase – actually *blame*. We have now turned our self-criticism completely outwards and projected it onto someone else. Finally, in phase four – *retaliation* – we use all kinds of rationalisations to justify that this person deserves to be punished.

So we have (unconsciously) removed ourselves from connection, empathy and compassion, and this can lead to us giving ourselves permission to harm another person or group of people.

A flash of green light as a positive interruption

When the light is red, we are absorbed in our mental constructs, which support and reinforce our 'Me First' intention. However, as soon as we catch a glimpse of a green light – of the reality in this moment and of our interconnectedness – we can see through our constructed red-light narratives. The flashes of green light interrupt these patterns and bring us back to reality.

These so-called positive interruptions can occur by chance, for example when the doorbell rings, the sun rises or we hear some music that intrigues us. When interrupted like this, we often see through our mental constructions ourselves. A thought or emotion can also positively interrupt our red light – such as the thought 'What if I didn't hear clearly and he actually wasn't talking to me?' Or, a positive interruption could also be a moment of awareness in which we notice – in either a kind, straightforward way, or often in an alarmed, ashamed and embarrassed way – that we were caught up in the red light. Sometimes this insight comes while we are meditating.

Also by doing Green Zone Communication exercises and joining a Green Zone group we are increasingly able to see through our own toxic certainties and red light patterns more quickly and clearly.

Our conversational partners can also call our attention to positive interruptions. This is very helpful because in red light mode we are not aware of our own patterns. Help from a green zone friend is not only helpful in the moment to help bring us back to reality, but can also help us gain insight into our triggers and patterns as they occur in our daily conversations.

Positive interruptions of the 'Heartless Mind' of aggression

The example below shows which interventions conversation partners can offer. Please note that a red light has a lot of momentum. It is not always possible to get the message across, and even if possible, it can sometimes take time, effort and a lot of patience.

Phase 1 of 'Heartless Mind': the complaint

Imagine that I have just banged my knee against a table at work. It hurts badly, but instead of being compassionate with myself, I start complaining to you: 'John should not have left the table there!' Now, as my conversation partner, you have the choice of agreeing with me, after which we can focus together on John, or to come back to the original pain and the bruise on my knee. For example, you could say something like: 'I see you have a big bruise on your knee, it must hurt a lot.' The antidote to complaint is to accept things as they are.

Phase 2 of 'Heartless Mind': divisiveness

Instead of focusing on my pain, I focus on John. I have turned my pain outwards, to avoid feeling it. I have driven a wedge between John and me, which reinforces my 'Me First' intention. As a partner in dialogue, instead of conspiring with me against John, you can choose to put yourself in John's shoes and say, for example, 'Others have done that too. I left it there just last week.' This blocks the way for me to use John as a target. The antidote to sowing discord is building a bridge.

Phase 3 of 'Heartless Mind': creating a target for your blame

In order to be able to bluntly accuse John, it is helpful to no longer view him as a human being of flesh and blood, but instead to reduce him to an object. In this way, I can allow or even convince myself to blame the object John for my experience of pain.

As my conversation partner, you can positively interrupt my mental constructions by saying something about John that portrays him as a living and feeling being, such as: 'I know John as someone who thinks carefully about what he is doing. Maybe he was having an off day'. In this way, John becomes a human being again instead of an object. The antidote to creating a target for our blame is to introduce the concept of compassion.

Phase 4 of 'Heartless Mind': retaliation

After constructing a story that John has caused my pain and isn't worth caring about, I can take the next step – I want retaliation for my pain. John deserves punishment. I can now hold the judgement that John should be fired.

Left alone, red light aggression has the tendency to slowly fall apart into other, more primary emotional states. Maintaining aggression requires constant mental fuel, in the form of red-light narratives. So there is a reasonable chance that when you do not feed my vengeful beliefs, I will start seeing flashes of the yellow light that underlies the red. If I have gone this far in my rationalisations, breaking through them is accompanied by feelings of guilt and shame. As my conversation partner, it is helpful – if possible – to adopt a compassionate attitude, particularly in this highly escalated phase. You can also invite the yellow light, by saying something like: 'I care about you. Suppose John is actually fired, you might be blamed for that'. Or: 'Punishing someone else won't take away your pain'. The antidote to retaliation is forgiveness and reconciliation.

Summary

We can help to break the escalation towards aggression by returning to 'We First' ('We Together'). Instead of allowing this series of intellectual rationalisations to suppress empathy and compassion, we return to the realisation that we are all human beings.

'Mindless Heart': when love turns into possessiveness

'Mindless Heart' justifies turning our power over to others to avoid abandonment

A 'Mindless Heart', like a 'Heartless Mind', is a red light pattern. Again, as with all red light patterns, the body, heart and mind are temporarily out of sync. But in this case we suppress the intelligence of the open mind and our emotions take over, grasping at sources of happiness and pleasure.

When we're connected to our green light, we enjoy our *'Mindful Heart'* and feel our innate unconditional kindness. This manifests in simple ways, like noticing that someone dropped something and immediately reaching to pick it up. Being in a moment of 'Mindless Heart' is the opposite of this: we become distracted by conditional unfriendliness. The red light of the 'Mindless Heart' is *conditional* because we only open up under certain conditions. The *unfriendliness* is in our attitude to ourselves: we doubt ourselves, suffer from an inner poverty and do not trust our own, inner source of love and beauty. As a result, we are constantly looking for external sources of beauty, joy and love.

With a 'Mindless Heart' we run away from ourselves and make ourselves dependent on others. We are afraid of being abandoned and need someone else to make us feel good. Emotionality prevails, there is no longer a sense of healthy boundaries. The other person has to behave in a certain way to compensate for our loneliness and insecurity. In a relationship, this leads to enmeshment, codependency and possessive behaviour, which our partner experiences as claustrophobic and oppressive.

In our green light state, it is our clear mind that balances our emotional life. But in a 'Mindless Heart' pattern, we are no longer paying attention to our mind. As a result, we can easily ignore reality and can get lost in idealization or even fantasies about how we wish things would turn out. We give away our power and our truth, in exchange for the illusion of safety, love and connection.

This may sound melodramatic, but we all regularly fall prey to the 'Mindless Heart' pattern. Every day in marketing and advertising messages, companies exploit our tendency to confuse our genuine need for love with our desire for momentary pleasure. One moment, we enjoy something beautiful. The next moment we *have to* possess it and we lapse into fantasy, deluding ourselves that we can hold on to one beautiful moment forever. This ignores the profound truth that pleasure comes and goes over time, and that real connection isn't just about feeling good.

The ever-changing nature of relationships

We can compare relationships and encounters with the four seasons. In spring, a friendship sprouts, in summer there is blossoming and intimacy, in autumn we say goodbye and in winter we are alone again. This can be a lifelong love affair, but also much shorter encounters. Esther Hasselman had the following experience with the four seasons.

'Once in London, I was standing at a traffic light trying to cross the street. On the other side stood a woman with the same purpose; we would pass each other in the middle of the street. It took some time, there was eye contact and a smile here and there. Finally, the light turned green and we walked towards each other. When we had approached each other, the woman looked at me and said in a friendly, very British way: 'That was quite a long wait,' to which I nodded and smiled; we had a moment of 'We Together'. Then we walked on and we each went our own way.'

Another example is the shared breakfast after which the family members go their separate ways, to school or work. The reality of life is that we cannot be together at all times, and that life includes distance as well as connection. In a 'Mindless Heart' state, we have temporarily lost touch with this reality and live in the illusion that we will always be together, and that any distance or difference means we've failed.

The value of disappointment

There come moments in life when the bubble bursts and our unrealistic expectations are confronted with reality. Here, disappointment can make our light turn yellow. As a partner in dialogue, we can be attentive and compassionate to what is happening in that moment. We show understanding for the disappointment, but we are also clear about the reality that love and loss unfortunately go together. Disappointments are often painful, but they are also very revealing. They bring us back to reality and make us aware that our expectations were not realistic. They provoke us to ask ourselves, 'How can I attune my human desire for warmth and affection so that I'm not counting on things others can never provide me with?'

The power of bringing our yellow light into a green zone

We've looked at two examples of red light patterns – the 'Heartless Mind' and the 'Mindless Heart'. We have been offered insight into how we close ourselves off from painful experiences, and we have been given some challenging but powerful tools to help ourselves or others to recognise these patterns, and to reconnect to reality – even if this is a painful reality. This works like peeling an onion, layer by layer.

We first move from the red light to the yellow light by gently meeting our fears and insecurities. In principle, we can do this ourselves – if we practise mindfulness, cultivate self-compassion and support ourselves through this vulnerable and sensitive experience. To help with this, we create our own, personal green zone, where we feel safe and can be completely ourselves.

In addition, we might form a green zone together with others – a social green zone, for example with a green zone friend or group – who are compassionately and protectively present, inviting us to remain present to the yellow light. The green zone forms, as it were, a safety net while we are in the groundless state of the yellow light. This makes it more bearable so that we can open ourselves to the wisdom that can unfold beneath the yellow light – which is that we are whole, coherent, wholesome and insightful – just as we are. This is true no matter how many things we need to learn, how many mistakes we've made or how many mindless emotional patterns we have yet to overcome.

Final reflections

Green Zone Communication is open to everyone. However, before we can participate in ongoing practice groups, it is necessary to have some basic training so that we can understand the principles and guidelines of Green Zone Communication, apply them genuinely and – if possible – reflect on them together with others.

Once we are familiar with these principles, we can apply them anywhere. It's important to remember that these are new skills that require practice and perhaps even some support to be able to implement them effectively – particularly with conversations that have a degree of emotionality or difference of opinion. It is therefore advisable to be careful with them, and to find one or more Green Zone friends with whom you make guidelines, so that there is permission to contradict each other in a compassionate manner, from the green light perspective of 'We Together.'

Conclusion

Green Zone Communication not only offers an optimistic view of people and human interaction but is also realistic in recognising the difficulties that communication can bring. Beginning with the vision that there is actually nothing wrong with us to begin with, communication in the green light can flow freely and naturally, and we can work together to attend to this and restore it if necessary.

The traffic light model provides a basis for monitoring what is happening during conversations. The principles of 'When the light is green: Go,' 'When the light is red: Stop,' and 'When the light is yellow: Be careful,' are simple enough to apply straight away.

In order to learn how to use these valuable tools, a number of online and offline training courses are available for a variety of people with different backgrounds in which we learn to apply the guidelines from this chapter step by step. There are certified Green Zone teachers and group leaders in Europe, and in North and South America, who facilitate Green Zone groups. See the websites in the resources table in the end of this chapter (Table 4.1).

Dialogue exercise

Find a Green Zone friend. Decide who will speak first and who will listen. The listener does not interrupt the speaker. The speaker describes themselves in terms of:

- *awake body (physical experiences, e.g. where they live, what they like to eat, etc.);*
- *tender heart (emotional life, e.g. 'I think humour is very important,' etc.);*
- *open mind (our relationship to ideas, beliefs, meditation and so on).*

Spend about three minutes on each of these topics. After ten minutes, switch roles. Finally, take ten minutes to talk together about whatever comes up.

Table 4.1 Resources

RESOURCES
Books:
• Susan Gillis Chapman (2012). *The five keys to mindful communication. Using deep listening and mindful speech to strengthen relationships, heal conflicts & accomplish your goals.* Boston, MA: Shambhala. (This is the basic book on Green Zone Communication).
• Chögyam Trungpa (2007). *Shambhala: The sacred path of the warrior.* Boston, MA: Shambhala. (Edited by Carolyn Rose Gimian: an accessible introduction to the shambhala tradition).
• Irini Rockwell (2012). *Natural brilliance – A Buddhist system for uncovering your strengths and letting them shine.* Boston, MA: Shambhala. (A handy book about the five Buddha families).
Videos:
• Webinar *Holding each other's hearts when families are not connecting* with Greg Heffron: see www.youtube.com/watch?v=4EOdSbX2GN8 (40 min).
• Webinar *Applying the three lights to families* with Greg Heffron: www.bit.ly/3LBtyQF (28 min).
Audios:
• Short exercise *Getting in touch with our natural communication system* with Greg Heffron: www.bit.ly/3H5pHlc (only audio) or www.bit.ly/3JvlFKs (with video).
Websites:
• www.greenzonetalk.com – Green Light Communications.
• www.mindfulcomm.org.
• www.whenconversationsmatter.com – website Chris Trani.
• www.goedgesprek.training/english/ – website Esther Hasselman.

Notes

1   The five yellow light fears are derived from the five so-called 'Buddha families' of Tibetan Buddhism, in which these five styles or energies are seen as fundamental building blocks of experience.

Each of these styles has a mindless, ego-oriented side (red light) and a healthy, connected side (green light). They also each exhibit a core fear (yellow light) which shapes their version of self-doubt. The five keys in Chapman's book *The five keys to mindful communication* (2012) are also inspired by these five energies.

The reference resources at the end of the chapter can be useful to explore them more fully. In this context, we'll limit our exploration to psychological reactions and responses in the present moment. And it will be helpful to keep in mind that no one person is limited to a single one of these energies.

The green light (mindful) state of the first energy, called *buddha*, has a natural affinity with spaciousness and engaged silence, allowing everyone their voice and experience. The red light (distracted) state is to be 'spaced out' and opposed to letting in experience. The yellow light fears that 'no space could ever welcome who I really am.'

The green light state of the second energy, called *vajra*, takes in the largest possible view with an affinity for honesty and clarity, helping everyone to remember what's real. The red light state falls into harsh criticism and coldness ('Heartless Mind'). The yellow light fears that 'I can never accurately perceive reality, and will always be careless and mistaken.'

The green light state of the third energy, called *ratna,* appreciates the richness and worthiness of every last person and experience, inspiring us all to celebrate fearlessly, beyond self-censorship. The red light state sees richness as limited, and hordes it, falling into greed and arrogance to try and bolster one's inner wealth. The yellow light fear is that one is worthless and fundamentally deprived of value.

The green light state of the fourth energy, called *padma*, is to flow with the coming and going of relationships with complete fluidity and warmth, allowing everyone to connect in their unique way and in their own time. The red light state is to mimic 'warmth' and 'connection' at all costs, which includes sacrificing or manipulating the truth ('Mindless Heart'). The yellow light is to fear that we are fundamentally unlovable and without our own inner warmth – so that a sense of connection must always be manipulated from an outside source.

The green light state of the fifth energy, called *karma*, expresses as the ability to sense cause and effect in real-time, and to adapt elegantly to issues and opportunities that arise, such that everyone progresses together. The red light is toxic competitiveness, where endless 'opponents' need to be out-strategized and suppressed. The yellow light fears that we lack the ability to work with life as it is, and that we are fundamentally powerless.

Different energies can work within a single individual, or show up within multiple people in a situation. Contemplating the green light power of each of these five energies can help overcome condemning any style or wishing it were different than it is, without minimizing shut down patterns or behaviours.

Chapter 5

Mindfulness and Communication
Creating a space to coexist

Edel Maex

> *Mindfulness is a quality of attention in harmony with wisdom and compassion.*

What is mindfulness? This is not a superfluous question, because recently there appears to have been much confusion surrounding this word. Mindfulness is a common word in the English language, often used to translate the Buddhist term *sati*, or more precisely, *samma sati*. *Sati* refers to the ability to bring one's attention to something, *samma* means harmony. *Samma sati* is an element of the Eightfold Path of Buddhism, a quality of attention in harmony with wisdom and compassion.

When Jon Kabat-Zinn was looking for a name for his stress reduction programme, he chose mindfulness. He used it as an umbrella term to honour the Buddhist origins of the meditation techniques he was teaching. Thus, the word 'mindfulness' became the name of a method as well as a tradition, depending on the context.

The programme was originally intended to help participants with stress reduction, but over the years it has been adapted to many other contexts. Nowadays we find mindfulness programmes in the prevention of depression, in education, in business and so on. The Mindfulness and Communication programme described in this chapter is one such development.

How things began

Mindfulness training is the central activity of the Stress Clinic in the Antwerp hospital where I work. The program started as a faithful copy of the MBSR program, but over the years it has become more and more my own program. It remained true to the original content and to the format of eight weeks of home practice. The programme, as it is now, has its own particular emphases, adapted to the context in which we are offering it.

In the original MBSR programme, the sixth session is dedicated to communication. This turned out to be an important theme: many of the

DOI: 10.4324/9781003262008-5

questions from participants, for example, in follow-up meetings, are about communication problems. It was also important to repudiate the common preconception that mindfulness is only about yourself. Mindfulness is not navel-gazing. It is rather a form of open awareness, directing the attention not only inwards but also outwards.

I noticed a tendency to add an increasing number of exercises to the original communication session in the MBSR programme until the session became overloaded. So I started thinking about a mindfulness training programme specifically for communication. Originally, the Mindfulness and Communication programme was conceived as a continuation of the stress reduction programme, but it has since come to stand alongside it, as an equal alternative approach to mindfulness. Many participants now start with the stress reduction programme and do the MBSR training as a continuation.

The communication programme was several years in development. There was a lot of hesitation and it was important not to create false expectations. If you ask someone with a communication problem 'What would have to change to improve the relationship?', the answer is usually 'The other person'. That answer may not actually be wrong, but it won't get you anywhere. Philosophising about how the other person should change is pointless because you simply cannot force change on another person. Mindfulness and Communication, on the other hand, is about what you yourself can do. The programme is intended to help you reflect on yourself, your own role and the ball that is in your own court.

Like all mindfulness programmes, Mindfulness and Communication is an open experiment. The real practice happens at home, at work, on the street and in all the communications you have. The communication programme doesn't tell you what to do. Mindfulness explores and makes visible. It offers more freedom of choice, without imposing a choice.

Our setting and participants

The programme was created in the context of the Stress Clinic, i.e. in a hospital, in a setting that is part of the psychiatric department. The Stress Clinic does not focus on major psychiatry, but on a wider range of stress-related problems, both psychological and psychosomatic although it is, of course, based on my own expertise as a psychiatrist. Very many psychological complaints are (at least partly) caused by stress, which in turn causes more stress, much of which has a relational cause. Many people in my practice carry a history of physical, sexual and/or psychological violence, sometimes very intense, sometimes subtle. The kindness of open attention, for yourself and for each other, is the direct antidote to that violence. That was my main motivation for introducing mindfulness in my work, and in expanding it to the Mindfulness and Communication programme.

The groups in the hospital are heterogeneous. Not everyone has the same traumatic history, and human suffering is not fairly distributed. However, the heterogeneity of the groups is an advantage as it means that people with a more difficult history can be carried by the group. Mindfulness is not a psychotherapy, but the two are complementary and can reinforce each other. Because mindfulness can force us to confront our own discomfort, it is sometimes necessary to organise additional, individual contact with a psychotherapist, so the personal story of the person in question can be adequately addressed.

Do you have a right to exist?

This is the key question that I have asked patients and participants countless times. The question is of course embedded in a conversation, but usually the other person immediately understands what I mean. The basis of all relational violence is that you are not allowed to just be as you are. Violence is subjecting the other person to your demands instead of recognising his or her right to be different. Mindfulness is very much about respecting your own right to exist.

The right to exist is also the basic principle of Mindfulness and Communication. If you think back to Jon Kabat-Zinn and MBSR, this is very similar to the principle of 'no fixing', or not meeting someone with the agenda of sorting them out or fixing their problems. It is about expecting that the other person accepts us as we are with all our quirks, faults and issues and about meeting the other person in turn with an acceptance of all their failings and limitations. So we expect the other to grant us the right to exist, and at the same time respecting the other person's the right to exist.

Three observations as a guideline

There are three observations that I have always used as a guide. They are rules of thumb, not absolute laws, but they often help me to understand human suffering and to assist participants in disentangling the knots they find themselves caught up in.

We treat ourselves and others as we have been treated

We have learned how to deal with ourselves. It is important to realise that we do not learn by what we are told, but by how we are told. If you preach to your child that he should have more respect, you are more like to teach him preaching than respect. It is the patterns of interaction that are passed on: dominating and being dominated, respecting and being respected. In this way, ways of behaving are passed on from generation to generation.

If you do not respect yourself, it is very difficult to teach your child respect. If you start demanding respect, you teach your child to demand or submit to a demand. If you live with a deep sense of self-respect, the chances are very high that you will naturally give the gift of self-respect to your child. We pass on what we are familiar with ourselves.

If this was the only observation, we would be pretty much stuck with our past. Fortunately, this is not set in stone because of the second observation.

We always have a choice

However, much we seem to be determined by our past, we can make a different choice at any time. It is important to become aware of that moment of choice, and that is what we practise in the mindfulness training. You start by following your breath and then at a certain moment you might notice that you are completely distracted. That is your moment of choice; in that moment you can return to your breath. You choose to be present with kindness to what is happening in your mind, and then you notice that you are beating yourself up again. That is your moment of choice; in that moment you can return to kindness.

However, your past has conditioned you, now you can choose to do things differently. Maybe you have to repeat the noticing and returning every second, a hundred times, a hundred thousand times, with unlimited kindness.

In listening to our desire, we can discover kindness

But what is it then, kindness, and where do I find it? How can I be kind to myself? How can I pass on what I have never received? May I ask another question: how do you wish to be treated when you are feeling vulnerable?

So far everyone has answered that question in the same way but in their own words. The answer is always along the lines of 'I don't want someone to tell me what I should do or have done, I don't want someone to start giving me good advice right away. I would like someone to just be there and listen, and treat me with kindness and respect'. In other words: I want to be accepted just as I am, including all my flaws. When people grant their own desire a right to exist, they arrive at that. So you know how you want to be treated and that desire is what will lead you to know what kindness is.

The communication compass

Two lovers sat on a park bench with their bodies touching each other, holding hands in the moonlight. There was silence between them. So profound was their love for each other, they needed no words to express it.

Samuel Johnson

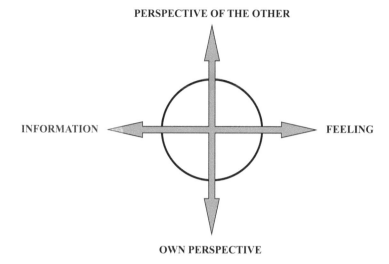

Figure 5.1 The communication compass.

Sometimes communication comes naturally. These are rare, gifted moments, as intense as they are fleeting. But sometimes communication is awkward and difficult. It seems as if we speak a different language and will never understand each other. The lovers on the park bench do not need words to understand each other, let alone words to talk about their communication. However, where communication is not so fluent, or if we want to learn certain forms of communication, we do need language.

In the Mindfulness and Communication method, we use the communication compass as a tool to talk about communication. Just like a real compass, it doesn't tell you where to go, but it helps you to orientate yourself.

Perspectives

The first axis in the communication compass is that of perspectives. Communication takes place between two different parties, each of whom looks at reality from a different angle. This results in two different perspectives on reality.

People often have difficulty thinking in terms of perspectives. We often think in terms of right or wrong. Western science owes its success to describing a reality which purports to be independent of perspective. We measure the weight of an object independently of the person who has to carry it. Five kilos might seem heavy to one person but light to another – although expressed in kilograms, the weight is exactly the same.

When we talk about communication, we have to give up this idea of objectivity. Reality is different for everyone. Reality looks and feels different from every perspective. Different perspectives are important, neither is superior to the other. It is these perspectives that are the raw material of all communication.

The first question you need to ask yourself in order to communicate well is therefore: what does reality look like for the other person? What would it be like to be in their shoes? The problem here is that we can never get a definitive answer to this question. We will never really know what it is like for the other person because we only have direct access to our own perspective. With this in mind, one might wonder whether communication is fundamentally possible, yet our experience is that people can meet each other on common ground while respecting each other's perspective.

Communication has two possible pitfalls in this area. The first is that you start seeing your own perspective as 'the truth' and remain blind to the perspective of the other. The second pitfall is that you become so absorbed in the other person's perspective that you lose sight of your own. As soon as one of the perspectives is given a monopoly position, communication shuts down.

Information and feeling

Question: 'Darling, have you called the plumber?'
Answer (irritable): 'Why do I always have to do everything on my own here...'

Who does not recognise this kind of situation? The second axis of the communication compass is that of information and feeling. The question in the example above has been formulated just by asking for information, but the answer is all about feeling. Information and feeling always occur together. Misunderstandings arise if they are mixed up, for example, if information questions are answered with an expression of an experience or vice versa.

In the example, we don't really have enough background to understand what's really going on. Perhaps it is a very simple request for information, but the partner has had a bad day or feels guilty. And maybe there is a hint of annoyance hidden in the seemingly innocent question, something like: 'You probably didn't call again'. Can you prevent situations like this? Well, of course not, but you can clarify them quickly if you are prepared to listen openly and without prejudice to the experience of the other person, from his or her perspective.

How the programme is structured

The Mindfulness and Communication programme consists of six three-hour sessions. These sessions can be given in six half-day sessions or three full-day sessions. It is important that there is sufficient time for practice between sessions. The homework is twofold: the participants do a guided or silent meditation of 15 minutes each day, and they also apply their observations from the sessions in their daily communications. That is where the real learning takes place.

The sessions consist of three elements. We start each session with a guided meditation, based on the idea that you cannot be present with the other person if you are not present yourself. The themes of the meditation link to the theme of the session. During the conversation after the meditation, the inquiry, the basics of mindfulness can be explained and clarified.

In each session we also do exercises in interaction, usually in pairs. These are small experiments with communication. The emphasis is not on success or failure, but on observing what happens, both to yourself and to the other. This observation is continued at home. In the following session, there is always the question: what did you encounter in your daily communications? The conversation, as in any inquiry, is not aimed at solving problems but at clarifying them.

This observation does not stop at the end of the programme. On the contrary, the participants have only just begun and in principle, they continue the observation throughout their lives. As with all mindfulness programmes, the exercises provide a tool with which they can continue to work. Different questions and themes are addressed in each session but the right to exist and the communication compass always underpin these.

- Session 1 starts with the question: how do you want to be treated?
- Session 2 is about the question: can you stay anchored within yourself when you are with the other person, or do you immediately lose all contact with yourself? How often does it happen, for example, that you say 'Yes' in a conversation and then realise afterwards that you did not really want to? We practise staying in touch with ourselves as well as with the other person, in order to give the other person a right to exist without this being at the expense of our own right to exist.
- In sessions 3 and 4, we introduce the communication compass by means of a number of exercises. The questions that arise are: can you really know the other person's perspective? When do you understand someone? To what extent is what happens in the conversation about information or feeling? How do you give information? When is it clear, and to whom is it clear? What is needed so that you are able to share your feelings?
- In session 5, we discuss the communication compass in more detail, based on the participants' own experiences. We practise using the questions: how do you bring in your own perspective? How do you make yourself known? What is violence?
- In session 6, we address the questions: what is compassion? How much can you handle? Where are your limits? In the last exercise, all the elements of the programme come together.
- The programme has an open ending. The participants apply what they have learned in their own lives.

An invitation to try out some exercises

In session 1, we do a small observation exercise in pairs, using two minutes for each step. After three times two minutes we reverse the roles so that both participants can experience the two different roles.

Exercise: The importance of attention

1. *Participant A tells participant B something. You are invited to talk about something simple, for example, what you did on holiday. Never tell more than you want to, guard your own privacy. B listens with open attention and gives A the space to talk, without immediately intervening.*
2. *A continues talking, but B stops listening. Distract yourself as a listener. You probably have your own holiday memories to think about, or just try looking at the ceiling giving the impression that even the ceiling is more interesting than what is being said.*
3. *Discuss among yourselves whether there was a difference between the first and the second situation. And if so, how was it different?*

During the discussion afterwards, a number of themes automatically come up that will be explored further in the next sessions. The first thing that becomes apparent, even in a small game like this, is how important attention is. Not just any attention, but the kind of attention that respects you and your right to exist.

Then there is the observation of your spontaneous reaction when you are no longer receiving attention. Some people immediately start doubting themselves, others get angry. Even though this is just a game, you experience real feelings. Some people fall silent when there is no more attention, or lose the thread of their story. Others try to re-establish contact and attract attention by adapting their story to that of the other person. And still others just carry on talking when they no longer get any attention, which is actually completely pointless.

The observations from the other role are also discussed. Where was your attention when you were listening? Did you disappear completely into the other person's story, or did you stay in touch with yourself? And what is it like not to listen when you are ordered not to? All observations are important. In the homework, the participants are instructed to keep observing themselves in their daily communications. What happens with your attention? And with the attention of the other person? What are your spontaneous reactions? Can you remain conscious of this, or do you get carried away automatically?

The central theme of session 2 is being present with yourself and the other. We build this up with a number of exercises. In principle you can do two things with your attention: you can move it, and you can broaden or narrow it. For example, in an exercise like the body scan, you can move your attention to each part of your body, starting with your toes and then moving to the sole of your foot, to your heel, your ankle …, but you can also broaden or extend your attention from your toes to your foot, your lower leg, your whole leg and so on. Below, I describe the steps of a short guided meditation on broadening attention.

Exercise: Meditation is not just directing your attention inward

1. *Sit comfortably, open and with dignity.*
2. *Bring an object that is meaningful to you into your field of vision.*
3. *Close your eyes.*
4. *Bring your attention to your breath.*
5. *Broaden your attention from your breath to your whole body.*
6. *Slowly open your eyes and widen your attention to include the object in your field of attention.*
7. *Expand your attention even further, so that your thoughts and feelings appear in your field of attention.*

This exercise also raises a number of essential issues in the follow-up discussion. To begin with, the question arises as to whether we meditate with the eyes open or closed. This exercise is the only mindfulness exercise in which I ask participants to close their eyes. Also in the first introduction of sitting meditation in the stress reduction programme, I prefer to meditate with the eyes open. Mindfulness is open awareness, so why close one sense? But I invite people to experiment with both possibilities.

People who have more experience with meditation and are used to closing their eyes often experience this exercise as strange. Meditating means for them that they close themselves off and turn their attention inwards. That is something different from open awareness. And of course, we don't normally close our eyes when communicating with other people.

Step 6 is crucial in this exercise. The experience of many participants is that as soon as they open their eyes, the attention is completely sucked into the image and the rest disappears. This is also how the magician's wand works: one hand waves the wand, while the other hand hides the egg in an inner pocket.

What often disappears when opening the eyes, is the contact with yourself, with your breathing, with your body. You are no longer present. That is why we usually repeat step 6. We close the eyes again and then open them very slowly so that we can be with ourselves and the image at the same time. In this way, you create a space of open attention in which both you and the environment are present and exist. In this space, you can also observe spontaneous thoughts and feelings in yourself, and remain present without losing yourself in them.

This exercise is a stepping stone to the next exercise, in which we do essentially the same thing, but this time in interaction with someone else. The important observation in the exercise and in the homework is: can you stay present?

Difficulties and pitfalls

Like all mindfulness programmes, the Mindfulness and Communication programme can bring us into contact with discomfort which can feel challenging and painful. It makes visible what is going well and where you are 'at the wheel', but it also shows you where things are going wrong and what is escaping your control. Communication is not enforceable. You can invite the other person, but not force them.

If the other person does not accept your invitation, you are left standing there with your good intentions. This can be all the more painful in intimate relationships, in relationships with your family and other people who are important in your life. Sometimes it becomes clear that the other person is not really prepared to recognise your right to exist and it becomes clear where all the pain, sometimes of years of it, is coming from. Mindful communication does not mean you always have to be sweet and nice; sometimes you have to clearly indicate your boundaries, and sometimes there is nothing left to do but protect yourself.

The programme is designed with the stories of people with serious traumas in mind. A traumatic past is therefore not a counter-indication for participation in the Mindfulness and Communication programme, but working with trauma does require special care and safeguarding. The focus on respectful communication can then be particularly challenging, for example, when someone's personal story is just too difficult to be handled within the scope of the programme. Such participants may need to have the opportunity to get extra therapeutic support outside the sessions.

The biggest pitfall is to moralise. People often hear an implicit obligation in what you say. If you speak about kindness, the question quickly arises: 'do I always have to be kind, like, even to my mother-in-law?' This pitfall does not only exist for participants; I also regularly hear mindfulness teachers use phrases such as 'You should...'. But even if you don't mean it like that, people often still hear what you say as a 'should'. Then you risk undermining your own message. Let the way you communicate be congruent with the content of what you are teaching.

Like all mindfulness programmes, the Mindfulness and Communication programme is offered with greatest kindness and utmost respect for the participant's perspective. Mindfulness opens up possibilities. It is up to the participant to freely accept or reject them, and to decide for themselves in each situation what he or she does with these possibilities.

A few final words

Mindfulness and Communication can be a valuable supplement to MBSR, or it can be a stepping stone to it. Like MBSR, the programme originated in the context of a hospital, but it can also be used in other contexts. It is my experience that in a business context, where communication is often an issue, it can provide a more accessible, focused and understandable access to mindfulness.

Table 5.1 Resources

RESOURCES
Books:
• Edel Maex (2006). *Mindfulness. In the maelstrom of your life.* Tielt: Lannoo.
• Edel Maex (2018). *What mindfulness is not. And what it is.* Tielt: Lannoo.
Audios:
• 3. Broadening the Field (Edel Maex).
• 4. Wish (Edel Maex).
Website:
www.levenindemaalstroom.be – website Edel Maex.

Chapter 6

Deep Listening

Transforming communication

Rosamund Oliver and Chantal Bergers

Introduction

There are few training courses that are purely about learning how to listen. *Awareness Centred Deep Listening Training (ACDLT®)*, offering training in *Deep Listening*, is one. Being able to listen well is an important skill when making meaningful connections with others. By simply listening with awareness and presence, we enable the other person to be more in touch with what is happening for them. This process of deeper listening, where the listener mirrors the speaker's process, supports another to either free themselves from difficulties, or deal with them more effectively. As Henri J.M. Nouwen (2006) states, 'True listeners no longer have an inner need to make their presence known. They are free to receive, to welcome, to accept. Listening is much more than allowing another to talk while waiting for a chance to respond.'

In Deep Listening, we bring our awareness into the present moment as we listen, giving compassionate attention to the other person and welcoming them into our very being.

Rosamund Oliver, who founded ACDLT, said, 'I deeply believe that simply listening to another person, without saying too much, is a natural human skill. It is something we can all do and is very beneficial and even healing for others. And I also believe that not enough knowledge of this skill is available in the world. It is not used enough. Not listening to each other creates fragmentation, and fragmentation creates division and misunderstandings in our families, communities and organisations.'

Chantal Bergers, a doctor and Senior ACDLT Trainer, describes her first experience of using this method: 'When, as an experienced GP, I first took this course, I was immediately struck by the simplicity and power of the method. I had just recovered from burnout, which was partly caused by thinking that I always had to solve everything for others. Here I learned something completely different.' As Dick Price, a student of Fritz Perls, the founder of Gestalt therapy, said, 'Trust process, follow process, and get out of the way.'[1]

DOI: 10.4324/9781003262008-6

I learned to let go, to trust the wisdom that is already present in every human being. My experience is that an attentive, accepting presence is often sufficient and offers a lot of space for people to come up with their own insights, realisation, or solutions. This generally has a much deeper and better effect than when I try to solve things for them. Also, I don't have to try so hard to ask good questions, to guide the process, to push people with words or to save someone, so I can listen in a more relaxed way. It doesn't mean that, as a doctor, I put my diagnostic and therapeutic skills aside. It's more that Deep Listening creates a kind of basis from which I work; and in this way it is much more than just an addition to my profession.

Participants in ACDLT training find that a simple exercise can be a very special experience. They feel profoundly touched when someone really listens; giving them space to explore what is happening inside themselves. A charity worker said after an ACDLT training: 'I have the feeling that it has been a long time since someone really listened to me. It was a moving experience, and it made me see and appreciate the power of deep listening.'

In this chapter, we explain how the programme came about, its strengths and for whom Deep Listening Training is suitable. This is followed by an explanation of the ACDLT method, with practical examples of Deep Listening in action followed by a contemplative meditation exercise that you can try out for yourself.

The origin of Awareness Centred Deep Listening

ACDLT was first developed in 2003 by Rosamund Oliver when asked by the matron of a local hospice for a training in deep listening for her staff, to enhance how they provided care and to build on their existing listening skills. Responding to this request, Oliver drew on her experience and training as a psychotherapist combining listening skills with contemplative practices from the Buddhist tradition. She developed a method that had immediate application not only in medical settings but also in a wide variety of professional organisations where listening is an essential part of the day-to-day work.

Deep Listening, focusing primarily on listening, is not a therapy, although it can be combined with therapeutic approaches and other types of listening. It brings together the person-centred approach of humanistic psychology, with Tibetan Dzogchen awareness meditation, and the Mahayana Buddhist emphasis on compassion. All these approaches are holistic and assume the basic beneficence of human nature (Ricard, 2015). Through meditations and exercises, Deep Listening reconnects the listener with the natural mind, which is innately peaceful, kind and compassionate. We extend our listening awareness from this core place within. This natural way of being is recognised in many different contemplative traditions. As Niamh, a hospital chaplain, explained: 'I found experiencing the Deep Listening and feeling its power, its spaciousness and deep connection with the listener very beneficial.'

Interest in Deep Listening Training has grown and there is now a substantial group of Registered ACDLT Trainers who provide both online and face-to-face training for universities, hospices, charities, as well as offering courses with open registration for professionals.

In Ireland, the five-day annual course at Dzogchen Beara is accredited for Irish GPs. In the Netherlands, this training is offered to doctors and GP trainers at universities in Amsterdam and Utrecht (VUMC and UMC). Citing its relevance, one GP trainer explained 'Through this course, I learned how to listen, and how to give space to the patient, to my trainees and also to give space to myself.' Courses are held in mindfulness settings, such as the Centre for Mindfulness in Amsterdam, and for professionals in Germany, the UK, the US and Spain.

In 2020, because of the pandemic, which initially prevented the possibility of face-to-face training, Deep Listening Training was offered for the first time online and this adaptation to online has been surprisingly successful.

The strength of the programme

One of the strengths of the programme is its cross-cultural appeal. Working at the level of pure listening, taking in all levels of what is being communicated, rather than predominating content, gives it a practical applicability of being effective in many different listening situations. It also functions well in professional settings where compassion in communication is needed. After attending a workshop in Berlin, a doctor said: 'My way of listening when I take a medical history becomes more aware and multifaceted when I employ and internalize the many aspects of Deep Listening and bring them into my meetings with patients and staff.'

Who is Deep Listening for?

Deep Listening is suitable for anyone for whom listening is a substantial and essential part of their work and who already has basic listening skills. Deep listeners could be psychologists, psychotherapists, doctors, nurses, social workers and chaplains. Also, many teachers, lawyers, managers, project leaders and other professionals who work with people are interested in applying more profound ways of listening in their work. For example, managers can bring Deep Listening into working with their interns as well as into conversations with management teams.

A number of participants have applied the method in their relationships with family members and friends. An Irish psychotherapist said to Oliver a year after she completed the training: 'Yes, it was certainly helpful for listening to my clients, but the most important thing was the positive effect it had right away on my listening to my mother. It completely changed my relationship with her.'

We might think that Deep Listening is for longer listening sessions and that we need to set aside a lot of time to really listen to someone, but this is not necessary. A person can feel totally heard in ten minutes or less. The method can be used not only in longer sessions (therapy, caregiving or coaching) but also in ten-minute sessions, such as in GP consultations and everyday care practice.

Deep Listening can also be used in non-speaking situations. Natalia Lane, a Bowen Technique Therapist, explains: 'The listener is present to "what is" and provides a compassionate, congruent, non-judgemental safe space for the speaker to say what's on their mind, without interruption or interjection, which allows truth to surface and for answers to be discovered for oneself. For me, I find it most useful in difficult situations, where words are rendered useless, where there is nothing to be said, it helps me to build the resilience not to flee when faced with difficulty and to avoid burn out. It has taught me to care and look after myself so that I can genuinely be there for the other.'[2]

What is Deep Listening?

There are two ways of listening. First, there is conceptual listening, where the attention is focused on hearing information. We focus mainly on what is being said, the content, the story and the topic. Secondly, we can listen, centred in awareness, and become present the full flow of what is being communicated. In this way, the listener can hear many different layers in the process of both spoken and unspoken communication. Unspoken communications are part of a subtler, deeper process that has not yet been explicitly expressed in the listening exchange. Listening, centred in awareness, also involves our being attuned to the other person, holding compassionate connection with them and their process of communication. By paying attention to the speaker's process, we are less likely to come up with solutions arising from our own agenda rather than the needs of the other person.

To hear another person, we need both ways of listening. We are usually skilled in the first way, but often need training and encouragement for the second way of listening. Deep Listening seeks to specifically address this need and build on existing listening skills.

The Deep Listening Model

Awareness Centred Deep Listening is a process and the model showing this has three connected core listening skills:

- Coming to embodied awareness
- Holding supportive presence
- Generating compassionate connection

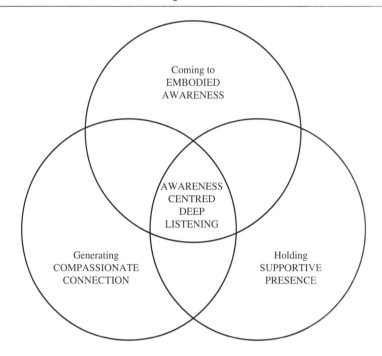

Figure 6.1 The Deep Listening Model.

These core skills are an innate capacity within every human being and are part of the process taking place while listening. So, we use verbs to describe how we experience them in action. When all three skills come together in the activity of listening, this is Awareness Centred Deep Listening.

Coming to embodied awareness

> *The body is clearly an instrument of physical processes, an instrument that can hear see, touch and smell the world around us. This sensitive instrument also has the ability to tune in to the psyche: to listen to its subtle voice, hear its silent music and search into its darkness for meaning.*
> Mathew (1998)[3]

We begin with the first core skill of coming to embodied awareness. Humans are embodied beings who are naturally aware because they are alive and conscious. Humans have a consciousness or mind which is embodied, as Daniel Siegel (2020) said, our mind is an embodied and relational process. Our consciousness depends on the existence of various processes taking place in the body. When we speak about mind, we also include 'heart,' the feeling or relational aspect of our mind which includes the communication an individual has with other beings in the world.

We experience embodied awareness when we fully come back into feeling our body. Jon Kabat Zinn calls this our own interiority, the experiencing of our own body and all our senses, including the mind. This means that we both feel our body's postures and movements (proprioceptive) and the various responses or emotional reactions we generate within ourselves with the corresponding physical sensations (interoceptive).

We often do not perceive our bodies at all. For example, if we are at work and have had a busy day, we may already be thinking about the meal at home and not feel the tiredness in our bodies. And during the meal at home, we often think back to our work and don't even taste what we are eating!

We usually do not realise this chronic lack of embodiment, because our own mind and the way we live constantly distract us. How aware are we of our body and our surroundings when we are typing a text or when we are reading a news article on our mobile phone?

Jon Kabat-Zinn puts it like this: 'With our mobile phones and wireless palm devices, we are now able to be so connected that we can be in touch with anyone and everyone at any time and do business anywhere. But have you noticed that, in the process, we run the risk of never being in touch with ourselves? In the overall seduction, we can easily forget that our primary connection to life is through our own interiority the experiencing of our own body and all our senses, including the mind, which allow us to touch and be touched by the world, and to act appropriately in response to it.'[4]

The importance of bodily awareness for listening

If we, as listeners, are not aware of our bodies, we become more easily distracted from the present moment and then we fail to hear what the speaker is saying. We may be entangled in thoughts and emotions arising within us. Maybe we actually want to share our own story and are waiting for a time to do so. Then we are no longer present to listen, we are no longer 'at home' in our body.

Another advantage of using this conscious body awareness is that our bodies become listening instruments, sounding boards for the verbal and non-verbal signals that the speaker sends. This capacity of embodiment was noted by Allan Schore (2012): 'To do this the clinician must access his or her own bodily based intuitive responses to the patient's communications.'

Chantal also writes about this. 'I can experience a very heavy feeling in my body when I talk to someone who is depressed. In this way, the sensations in my body can be an antenna for what may be going on with my conversation partner. It is important to recognise that these physical sensations come from the other person and do not "belong" to us. If we are not aware of this and do not "channel" these feelings, a day of listening can be tiring, and in the long run can even lead to burnout.'

How do we develop bodily awareness?

Because the mind naturally lives in our body, we only need to bring it back to its natural home using awareness. We can do this by using breath to connect to our body or by using awareness to quickly travel through the body, simply noticing what is happening. Such body scan methods are also adapted for use in mindfulness and relaxation training.

In Deep Listening, for increasing embodiment, we apply a tool called the Listening Centre. To begin listening, the listener chooses a physical place in his or her body, to serve as an anchor for their awareness. Gradually, they expand this awareness outwardly, to include the other person. The starting place can be the abdomen, navel, heart area, throat, forehead or somewhere else in the body.

Holding supportive presence

Coming to embodied awareness is an important skill in listening. However, just being embodied does not create Deep Listening. Additionally we need to bring in holding supportive presence, the second core skill. A person can be very embodied, in his or her body, such as an athlete or dancer, without being available to listen in depth to another person. To be a deep listener, we also need to hold supportive presence for another person. As we expand our awareness to include the other person, we hold an intention to stay present and be available to listen. Jon Kabat-Zinn (2018) describes this skill:

> *To be present is far from trivial. It may be the hardest work in the world. And forget about the 'may be.' It is the hardest work in the world - at least to sustain presence. And the most important, when you do fall into presence - healthy children live in the landscape of presence much of the time - you know it instantly, feel at home instantly. And being home, you can let loose, let go, rest in your being, rest in awareness, in presence itself, in your own good company.*

Our awareness then follows the speaker from moment to moment, while at the same time being aware of what is happening in ourselves. If we are not present and listening, our speaker will notice this, and this will affect how they communicate with us, they may disclose less, or even stop talking altogether about whatever they wanted to talk about.

> *From experience you know that those who care for you become present to you. When they listen, they listen to you. When they speak, you know they speak to you. And when they ask questions, you know it is for your sake and*

not for their own. Their presence is a healing presence because they accept you on your terms, and they encourage you to take your own life seriously.

Henri J.M. Nouwen (2004)

How do we practice being fully present?

As listeners, we practise both mindfulness meditation and awareness meditation to develop greater presence, more stability of mind and greater awareness. This is part of listening to ourselves. Mindfulness meditation focuses on the body and breath, which helps to quieten our mind and body. Whenever we get distracted by thinking and feelings, and become less present, we gently bring our attention back to the here and now using our body and breath as an anchor. This is mindfulness meditation. We can integrate the presence gained from this mindfulness meditation to help us be present when listening to another. When the mind quietens and we are less distracted, we let this focused attention expand and drop any meditation technique, just sitting with open awareness in the present moment. This is awareness meditation.

When holding supportive presence, the listener naturally rests his or her mind in open awareness of whatever is happening in the listening field and silently connects with the other person with this open awareness without holding an agenda or asking questions. A listening field is the space that naturally arises when people come together with the intention of listening. It is a physical and at the same time a subtle and energetic space in which both verbal and non-verbal information is shared and exchanged between the speaker and the listener. We do this while staying *with* the physical experience of embodied awareness at the same time. Schore (2012) describes this as follows: 'The intersubjective field co-constructed by two individuals includes not just two minds but bodies.'[5]

When listening, open awareness means that we can both pay attention to what the speaker is communicating and at the same time be aware of the many other things taking place in the listening exchange. Open awareness includes spaciousness which can be correlated to the space held by the listener that allows the listening process to take place. Holding space is recognised as a valuable part of deeper communication.

An exercise we can do to train in open awareness is the *Five-Minute Method*. A description of this is at the end of this chapter.

Open awareness in action

When we apply open awareness in Deep Listening, we are actively present to three things:

- Being present to ourselves
- Being present for the speaker
- Being present in relation to the listening environment

BEING PRESENT TO OURSELVES

If we want to be really present for the other, we need to be present for ourselves first of all. Our self-enquiry about being present for ourselves might include some of these questions. What is happening in myself? What do I feel? What am I thinking? How can I, in addition to caring for the other person, also care for myself as a listener? Becoming being aware of what is happening inside ourselves helps us to approach others in an authentic and open way.

When we bring our attention to ourselves, we allow what the other person is saying to enter us. The speaker can then see that his or her story is really heard by the listener and the listening becomes more reciprocal and equal. Moreover, being aware of ourselves ensures that, while listening, we also detect our own needs as a listener, and this helps us to maintain a balance of self-compassion and care.

BEING PRESENT FOR THE SPEAKER

The listener being present for the speaker means that we are available to listen to him or her. We actively choose to remain present for the speaker while listening; we do not go off elsewhere with our minds. Of course, there will be times when we get distracted; that's quite normal. But when that happens, when we become aware of it, and without criticising ourselves, we just bring our attention back to the other person.

Because we emphasise the importance of being present to ourselves, in Deep Listening we do not focus *all* of our attention on the other person during listening, we are also aware of what is happening inside ourselves at the same time. To begin listening, we make contact with our Listening Centre, placing attention on a physical place in our body from which we expand our listening awareness to make contact with the speaker. As part of this, we consciously bring awareness to what is happening between ourselves and the speaker. And from time to time we bring awareness back to ourselves, noticing how we are responding, noticing how the body is reacting to what is being said. This is an exchange taking place between the listener and the speaker: subtle and non-subtle information; an energetic, emotional and even physical process. This exchange is described as a flow like a figure of eight, the eternity sign. Attention over time is roughly placed equally on myself and on the speaker, although this may vary depending on what is happening during the listening.

BEING PRESENT IN RELATION TO THE LISTENING ENVIRONMENT

By paying attention to the environment, the listener holds a safe space for the speaker. The listener checks whether the environment facilitates listening sufficiently. Simple practical questions are: 'Am I at the right distance from the speaker? Is it better to sit opposite him or beside him? Would it be good to take a walk together? Can I choose how to arrange the environment to support the speaker?'

Generating a compassionate connection

By listening with calm and understanding, we can ease the suffering of another person.

Thich Nhat Hanh (2006)

The combined core skills of coming to embodied awareness and holding supportive presence are not enough because they do not naturally make listening beneficial. *Deep Listening* also requires a third core skill, generating compassionate connection. This ensures the compassionate intention of our listening connection and that the listening is kindly and ethically directed for the benefit of the speaker.

Compassion is the wish to relieve suffering and its causes, coupled with the urge to act in order to do something about it. Compassion is sometimes called 'the inability to bear someone else's suffering.' So, it is not only a feeling of friendliness for the person in pain, or a clear recognition of their need, it is also an ongoing, and practical determination to do what is necessary and possible to alleviate their discomfort.

So, compassion is more than just empathy. It includes a strong cognitive element of reason. It is an attitude that can be directed towards everyone, including ourselves. It is very much about respect for the other person and is not pity.

Compassion can therefore be seen as a combination of empathy and common sense; providing an ability to see what is best in a given situation. Compassion requires the capacity to understand the feelings or emotional states of others, which includes two major components: affective empathy, which is the ability to experientially (i.e., emotionally and viscerally) share the affective states of others; and cognitive empathy, or the ability to take in the mental perspective of others and make inferences about their mental or emotional states (Cox et al., 2012; Shamay-Tsoory, 2010).

Or to put it another way, as Nelson Mandela once said: 'A good head and a good heart are always a formidable combination.'

Empathy arises because we can make a connection with the feelings and experiences of another person. This is inbuilt before we ever become conscious that we can do this. For example, most babies can pick up and even mirror another baby's emotions without knowing they are doing so. This is not empathy as it is unconscious emotional contagion. As adults we can continue to share this connection and mature it into empathy, experiencing another's emotions while at the same time knowing that they have come from the other person.

Empathy is an important part of compassion; however, it does not have the same neurological responses as compassion. Compassion has an empathic component; however, for compassion, the essential addition is to have an authentic desire to identify what action or response is needed to help alleviate pain or difficulty. As Paul Gilbert (2010a) wrote: 'This ability to have empathy for difference, to be open to diversity, to work hard at thinking about how other people may differ from you is a key step on the road to compassion - and it's not always easy.'

Research shows that only responding empathically to communications, perhaps with a desire to rescue or fix without maturing it into a compassionate response, can contribute to burn-out. The listener experiences similar physiological responses as the speaker which can be exhausting. Generating compassion instead may lead a listener to take a step back to assess what is best needed, and after the listening has finished to let go of the effect of empathic responses and not take these on. Compassion, according to social neuroscientist Tania Singer, can help us not become overwhelmed by emotions or stressed when we listen to someone recounting an experience of pain and suffering (Singer & Klimecki, 2014).

Empathy and compassion rely on different biological systems and brain networks, and the response of compassion, involving a different part of the brain, still retains the listener's own well-being (Singer & Bolz, 2013).[6]

Compassionate responses allow us to stay connected and at the same time can best protect us from burnout. By applying the response of generating compassion, listening thus becomes energizing rather than exhausting, which is important if listening is a major part of our activity or work.

A Dutch doctor said: 'I wish that this kind of training was more available in medical schools. By discovering this listening method, I now experience myself, others and my environment in a very different way. This method is very useful in my work as a GP. The skills are very helpful and bring more joy and quality to my work. I learn to "recharge" myself after work and not to get burned out.'

Compassion lies at the essential heart of a deep listening relationship. When we have compassionate responses, we connect with the speaker. It is compassion, according to Margreet van der Cingel (2014) and Bernard Lown (1998), that improves the quality of our care. In addition, we have the desire to alleviate any pain or difficulty through listening, supported by our presence. Generating compassion, we do not judge our speaker, rather we create a safe environment in which they feel accepted and heard, perhaps for the first time.

How do we create a compassionate connection?

Compassion is innate, and so the care that arises from generating it, is naturally compassionate. As Paul Gilbert (2010a) writes, our brains are built for compassion. 'By the time of humans, our brains have evolved to be caring and to need caring to such an extent that the way they shape and wire themselves throughout life, the pattern of their interconnections, is significantly influenced by the affection, love and care they receive. Parental caring not only soothes children when they're distressed, but it helps them to understand and come to terms with how their minds work; they can talk about their feelings and things that have happened to them. Knowing that they exist in the mind of another as a loved person stimulates their soothing/contentment system and makes their world feel secure. This is the way our brains are built. We depend on care and love.'

However, although we have compassion within us, we don't always experience ourselves being compassionate. There are listening situations in which it is more difficult to feel compassion for the other person, for example, if they have done something we condemn or if they are unfriendly or hostile to us. So how to generate compassion? Even if we are not able to experience compassion, we can still wish for something good to come out of the listening and this good intention is the beginning of compassion. Another way is to resolve to keep an open mind and enter the listening session with no agenda and with no specific desired outcome. With compassion, at the end of the session, we find ourselves freer of judgements about whether our listening was successful or a failure. We are flexible and open, about what is shared with us. By bringing in compassion, being able to let go of fixing or rescuing, we don't become overwhelmed by any painful issues the speaker shares with us, for there is no pressure or expectation that we can resolve those issues. Instead, we just stay present and listen. A British psychologist working with the terminally ill-explained, 'I use Deep Listening with my clients, particularly those who are very ill. The method grounds me and when using it I find that I don't have to talk or take actions.'

Compassion exercises

Many people find that compassion arises naturally with us when we let the mind rest in natural awareness through meditation. This provides a natural listening mind. In addition to meditation, our training includes explicit exercises for cultivating compassion, for example, 'Seeing the other as another me,' a practice directed both towards ourselves and towards others. This type of reflection creates more understanding, acceptance and openness towards others and also of ourselves as a listener. We can also extend these practices towards people for whom we find it difficult to have compassion.

Chantal offers an example from her own experience. 'I remember going into the room of someone who had problems with feeling dependent and who often took it out on me and others. I tried to put myself in his shoes before I went in to listen to him. I asked myself: What could be going on for this man? What would it be like for me to be so dependent on my caregiver for my daily needs? And what does this person really need to support them now? This helped me to open up to this man, to feel compassion and understanding instead of irritated and judgmental, to not take his reactions so personally.'

A story from Chantal from everyday practice

'I came to a nursing home as a carer and had to look after a patient with MS who was steadily deteriorating. She could no longer speak. She regularly expressed her unwillingness to eat, but when offered food on a spoon, she often ate it anyway. This made the caregivers very uncertain about whether they should offer food or not? Her son also did not know what to do with the situation. Was his mother letting him know that she didn't really wish to eat anymore? Did she wish to die? Or was there something else going on?

I went to her room, which was very sparsely furnished. There was no chair next to her bed on which I could sit to get to her eye level. I introduced myself to her and said that I would like to talk to her and asked her if that was OK. She nodded. I saw that there was a heavy armchair in the corner and dragged it next to the bed. I thought briefly of my intention, my wish that my listening would bring something good to her and to all concerned.

She looked at me expectantly with bright eyes. I connected with my listening centre and extended my awareness to her, and at the same time listened within myself. There I noticed a certain expectation: I was hoping she would give me clear answers. I decided to let go of this expectation. Come what may. This brought me peace. As she could not talk, I asked her questions, to which she could then nod or shake her head. It was a beautiful conversation, although she couldn't utter a word. She made it crystal clear to me that life was no longer meaningful to her in this way. That it would be good if it would end, but that it didn't necessarily need to happen today or tomorrow. She realised that her end would come sooner if she often refused to eat and that would be okay.

But each time she wanted to make the choice to eat or not eat herself, so she did not want the nurses to stop offering her food. The "conversation" did not last much longer than fifteen minutes. There were also moments of silence, moments of natural rest.

I felt her trust in me, someone she had not seen before. A trust which I felt was nourished by my full attention, by moving the heavy chair to her bed so that I could look at her while being at the same height, and not talk down to her. These are small but essential things. I see you and I hear you, and your story matters. A week later she passed away peacefully.'

A story from Rosamund

'Deep listening, offered as a part of regular treatment in health care can support people to hear themselves more deeply. This can allow them to find more inner space to consider how they might be caught up in their unhappiness and even consider changes. For several years, I was working in old age psychiatry in Homerton Day Hospital in East London. I worked as a psychotherapist, coming in once a week to listen to people who had suffered debilitating loss through bereavement. The listening took place both in one-to-one sessions and in a bereavement group. There I met Henry, a lovely 82-year-old man, who cut off emotionally after the death of his wife, to whom he had been happily married for over 50 years. In cutting off, he was simply using a strategy that he felt had served him well throughout his life to cope with any big change and loss such as serving in the Second World War. When I met him this method of coping was "working" to such an extent that he could easily deny any feelings about his loss. It also left him with a disabling depression, sometimes unable to move for several days, and this brought him into non-residential psychiatric care. While I listened and said very little, he mostly wanted to talk about his great love for his wife and about what she had meant to him. This was important to acknowledge but the continual repetition of this also felt quite stuck. However, I just listened to the same story several times, letting him take the lead, while I followed and listened. Occasionally I asked him to say more or sometimes we sat in silence together. I had to trust the process that was happening although nothing seemed to be changing much. However, after a few sessions of saying he felt no great loss, something shifted inside him.

One day, after an extra-long period of silence, he took a risk and spoke about how he had been very distressed by his wife's long and painful final illness. And how much he felt unable to help her while spending many hours visiting her in hospital. In this way, he gradually began to be aware of his feelings about losing his companion and allow them through. The following week he found the courage to express this feeling of helplessness to members of a bereavement group. In return, he was then able to hear and receive reflections from other members of the group about how caring he had been as a husband. Shortly after this opening up, he decided to take up an offer of accommodation from his sister-in-law and move outside London to live with her, an offer he had previously been very dismissive about. Thus, if both the listener and the client can trust the process of deep listening, it may support finding a way to move on, even after a great loss. This can release fresh energy which can be used to explore how to live a fuller life again.'

The Five-Minute Method

To conclude here is a meditation exercise that you can do at home which includes all three core skills: the Five-Minute Method. During this five minute meditation, which we can do with our eyes open, we try to be fully aware and present. We are just in our natural being, present in our body, in the here-and-now, without distraction. This exercise is based on the one that Oliver originally described in *The healing power of meditation* by Andy Fraser (2013). It is inspired by meditation instructions from the Tibetan Buddhist tradition. It can be done in three steps: (1) Bringing our mind home (body awareness). (2) Releasing and becoming present (letting go of any physical or mental tension). (3) Resting in our natural mind (spacious and naturally compassionate).

Exercise: The five-minute method

Step I: Bringing our mind home
With eyes open, and looking down in front of us, we begin by sitting quietly and bringing our awareness to our body and to our breath. We breathe naturally. We are simply watching the coming and going of our breath and becoming lightly aware of our body. This helps us to arrive in our own body and be more present in the here-and-now. We are just feeling our body by making contact with the cushion or in the chair. We are being aware of our bodily sensations, our breath, thoughts and feelings. We accept these just as they are, without judgement. We do this quiet practice of body and breath awareness for about a minute.

Step 2: Releasing and becoming present
We continue, with this simple awareness, letting our thoughts settle. We are not following thoughts of the past, thinking of things that have already happened nor thoughts of the future, by anticipating what is still to come. At the same time, we are letting go of any 'holding on' and tension we feel. Just letting both the thoughts and any physical tightness release, in the same way, that we would open up a clenched fist by relaxing our hand. We can focus on our out-breath as we let go, releasing any tension we feel in our body or mind as we breathe out. Whatever thoughts or emotions arise, we just let them come and go, like waves in the ocean, simply being aware of being in the here and now. The thoughts are simply waves of the ocean of our mind. The secret is not to think about our thoughts, but to let them flow, without commentary. We do this practice of letting go of any physical or mental tension for about two minutes.

Step 3: Resting in our natural mind
As we continue to watch our breath coming and going, we find we experience more spaciousness and openness. We can do this while at the same time, being kind to ourselves, kind to any thoughts or feelings or body sensations arising as we allow our mind to settle and come to rest naturally. We let go of any method of meditation, such as observing our breath, and let our mind rest as much as possible in this state of openness, natural peace, and awareness, where the essence of compassion can arise. This is how we can connect with our natural listening mind. We can do this practice of resting spaciously and naturally compassionate for another two minutes.

Completing the practice
At the end of the meditation exercise, we take a moment to check how we are doing. How does it feel after doing this method? Does 'being aware' feel natural and relaxed? This is the atmosphere we are trying to bring into this exercise, this feeling of naturalness. When we finish the Five-Minute Meditation, we can then try to bring this feeling and experience of awareness into our subsequent daily activities and even our listening.

If we do this exercise even for five minutes every day, over time we will begin to feel more peaceful, and more in touch with our natural self. And we can then bring this experience in as a support when we listen.

Conclusion

We hope that by reading this account you have been inspired by this method. Many people have already taken *Deep Listening Training* designed to transform communication using their innate natural skills. Deep Listening supports listeners to develop a greater capacity to connect with the presence, awareness and compassion coming from the core of their being and to hold a safe compassionate listening space, without judgement, where another or others can truly express themselves and be heard.

With its potential for resolution, transformation and breakthrough, our listeners and ACDLT Trainers are now passing the method on to others every day in their work and life. We are working together to create a Deep Listening community, welcoming anyone who takes our courses to join. Listeners can contribute to bringing more mindfulness, awareness and compassion into society, ensuring that every person whoever they are can truly be heard. Deep Listening envisions a world where every person, organisation and community can benefit from the power of connected, open and supportive listening.

Sources underlying the ACDLT method

ACDLT uses elements of practical understanding drawn from humanistic psychology, particularly Carl Rogers' person-centred approach (1951, 1977) and Neo-Reichian body-centred psychotherapy. This contemporary approach to the importance of embodied relationship is combined with traditional elements of reflection and contemplation derived from the Buddhist tradition that are designed to bring more present awareness and develop greater compassion through practice of the methods. This understanding was introduced to the West by such teachers as the Dalai Lama, Thich Nhat Hanh (2005, 2006), Chogyam Trungpa and others. Mindfulness and awareness meditation exercises derived from this tradition are now used widely across the world within health services and in many other organisations, including corporate business. In the UK, the National Institute of Health and Care Excellence (NICE) recommends mindfulness training, as developed through the work of Jon Kabat Zinn and others, in the treatment of recurring depression, to help prevent relapse. Many of these traditional resources have been actively researched and then applied in the work of psychologists, scientists, and physicians, such as Daniel Goleman (1995); Jon Kabat-Zinn (1990); Zindel Segal et al. (2013); Paul Gilbert (2010b) and Paul Ekman (2008). The methodology of developing greater bodily awareness comes from exercises that have their basis in the tradition of neo-Reichian body-oriented psychotherapy, and we also use many elements from the Focusing method (Cornell, 1996; Gendlin, 1982).

Table 6.1 Resources

> ## RESOURCES
>
> **Books:**
> - Rosamund Oliver (2013). Being present when we care. In: A. Fraser (Ed.), *The healing power of meditation: Leading experts on Buddhism, psychology, and medicine explore the health benefits of contemplative practice* (pp. 176–191). Boston, MA: Shambhala.
> - Rosamund Oliver, (2013). Learning to listen: The benefits of deep listening training. *Article View Magazine, 7, 28–31.* (Available by email from: info@deeplisteningtraining.com).
> - Sandra Evans & Jane Garner (editors, 2004). *Talking over the years, a handbook of dynamic psychotherapy with older adults.* London: Routledge. (Rosamund Oliver and Erdinch Suleiman have written Chapter 18 'Bereavement' in this book).
>
> **Audios:**
> - 5. The Five-Minute Method – short version (Rosamund Oliver).
> - 6. The Five-Minute Method – extended version (Rosamund Oliver).
>
> **Website:**
> - www.deeplisteningtraining.com – website ACDLT® providing information about Deep Listening Training courses and Registered ACDLT trainers.

Beyond Words (verse 6)

Yes, I listen to whatever makes you talk
or stop what you are doing.

I listen in my silent heart
to the gaps in sound

as you breathe out
and before you reach

for breath again.
Sometimes the only place

we can agree
is beyond words.

Mary Branley[7]

Notes

1 See www.the-heros-journey.com/gestalt-according-to-dick-price.html. See also the interview with Dick Price at www.esalen.org/page/dick-price-interview.
2 Online blog 'Deep Listening Intensive – with Rosamund Oliver' from Natalie Lang, January 2019. See www.bowentechniquenorwich.co.uk/2019/01/24/deep-listening-intensive-with-rosamund-oliver.
3 Quarterly, 66, 219–241. Mathew, M.A.F. (1998). The body as instrument. *Journal of the British Association of Psychotherapists, 35, 17–36.*
4 Being Connected Within. Accessed May 11, 2020, from www.awakin.org/read/view.php?tid=536.
5 Here is a story to illustrate the difference between practising mindfulness and open awareness. A meditation teacher asked a student to walk up the stairs with a bucket filled to the brim without spilling any water. The student was very careful and concentrated and managed to bring the bucket up without spilling a drop. When he reached the top, the teacher asked, 'And what colour was the wallpaper on the wall next to the stairs? The student had no answer to this. He had concentrated so hard that he had not noticed his surroundings at all. The trick is to keep our attention on the bucket (mindfulness), and at the same time not to lose our awareness of what is happening in the environment (open awareness).
6 This ebook can be downloaded freely on www.compassion-training.org.
7 Verse 6 from *Beyond words* by Mary Branley, written after attending a Deep Listening Intensive. This poem was published in 2009 in her second collection of poetry called *Martin let me go.*

Chapter 7

Experiences with Open Dialogue

Mindfulness and the dialogic practice, on the way to insight

*Russell Razzaque, Heleen Wadman,
Kwok H. Wong and Olaf Galisch*

When we were first asked to write a chapter about Open Dialogue (OD) for this book, we immediately saw this as a great opportunity to generate more awareness for the necessity of a dialogical space within the mental health services. This first enthusiastic reaction was followed by months of deliberation and consultation. After all, OD has been seen from various perspectives. On the one hand, there is a strong theoretical framework from philosophy, sociology and psychology, but on the other hand, this approach also has a very practical side. In addition, we can see dialogue as a way of life that emphasises our shared humanity in a world in which systems and frameworks often appear to be dominant. In short, we did not know where to begin. So we decided to present four different perspectives.

- Olaf Galisch provides insight into the development of his practice as a psychiatrist. In it, he illustrates a search for an approach to making contact with clients despite symptoms of one or more mental illnesses.
- Kwok Wong gives a more technical description of OD and describes the connection with mindfulness.
- Heleen Wadman shares her own story of lived experience of mental illness and describes how she slowly found a way to relate to it. It is a story which clearly shows the need for a more dialogical approach to the mental health services.
- Russell Razzaque writes about how OD has been further developed by the addition of mindfulness training and peer workers in the UK. He is now involved in the largest, multi-centre randomised trial to date.

My introduction to OD – Olaf Galisch

I began my training as a psychiatrist in the 1990s. At first talking to patients felt a little strange. What questions should I ask in order to get a precise answer, an appropriate diagnosis and suitable treatment? My opinion was that you had to be able to get to the heart of the matter as precisely as

DOI: 10.4324/9781003262008-7

possible. This is what I saw as the art of the psychiatrist: not letting yourself be distracted by the broader stories. The question is though, how precise is the psychiatrist's scalpel? In the 1990s, there was great hope for the rapid development of effective treatments for mental disorders. Antipsychotics and antidepressants came onto the market promising fewer side effects and better results. Cognitive behavioural therapy became very popular because of its structured approach.

In the course of my first contact with clients, I soon gained the impression that I had little control over the conversation. The clients' answers did not fit into my scheme of diagnostic thinking and I felt we didn't understand each other. That's why I started to study the emerging methodology of psycho-education, to explain mental health problems to clients and their loved ones. It was an attempt to find a common language, but unfortunately it didn't work as well as I had expected. I had the impression that many things were left unsaid. In conversations with colleagues, I heard that psycho-education might be too complicated for this group, because of so-called negative symptoms such as loss of speech and apathy in clients, so I began thinking it was not my fault, perhaps it was simply the wrong target group.

After these psycho-education sessions, family members of clients often came to me and talked about their experiences. I immediately felt how important and enriching these stories were. At one point, a father asked if I would put the education sheets aside for a while. He had already listened to the explanations of professionals many times before and now he wanted me to listen to his story. I did, and I noticed that I did not have to do much. Just listen with attention, without reacting immediately. It sounds so simple, but it is a challenge just to listen and not to immediately seek explanations and offer solutions.

Many mental health institutions in the Netherlands are looking for recovery-promoting methods. The film Open Dialogue by Daniel Mackler (2011) about an alternative Finnish treatment for psychotic illness sparked my curiosity and in 2015, staff from eight Dutch mental health institutions went on a working visit to England, where this Finnish approach had already been implemented and developed further. We were very enthusiastic and decided to introduce this approach in the Netherlands as well.

The organisation of OD

OD is not new. It seems that with this way of listening and speaking we have rediscovered something that has always been there, especially in cultures that are focused on awareness and living in connectedness with others. OD has been developed out of the system theory approach. Unlike in many Western approaches, where the focus is on the autonomy of the individual, systemic theory always includes the client's network.

Just as in other European countries in the 1970s and 1980s, there were developments in Scandinavia to make psychiatric care available in the community. In Norway, for example, teams of various disciplines were set up, in which an important starting point was that they should also focus on the client's relationships and not deprive their network or environment of control. These teams attended systematic training courses and some were particularly fascinated by the 'Milan School' as a system theory methodology because of its attentive, careful, respectful and positive way of asking questions. Tom Andersen (1991), identifies two important insights in his further development of this method.

Exploring openly in dialogue can actually promote healing

Often no intervention by the therapeutic team is necessary, because the conversation itself can have positive effects. OD assumes that problems often have to do with processes that have come to a standstill, and that the conversation sets these processes in motion again.

The focus of the therapeutic team, therefore, lies more on the process and less on the result. In OD there is no object, game or structure that needs to be changed by therapy. There are several participants, the dialogue is a polyphony of several voices. Polyphony means that everyone has their own point of view, their own understanding of themselves and their environment; there is not one truth. Language is not reality, but it is created in a process of exchange between the participants in network conversations. This process not only takes place outside of ourselves but also in the inside, as a dialogue between our own perspectives.

Keeping all options open

The second insight has to do with the request for help from the client and his or her network. Andersen advises not to answer the question directly, but to let the whole system participate in exploring and reflecting on the request for help. The attentive, slowing down, searching, questioning and hypothesis-forming attitude of the therapists created more room for openness and diversity in the thinking of the network itself and this process produced several answers to the request for help. Getting to a diagnosis and medication too quickly closes the conversation and the path to making sense of things.

The experience of allowing silence and being able to express 'not knowing' as a therapist was eye-opening. The networks' experiences refuted the idea that not giving ready-made answer results in poor care and self-neglect. This 'new' approach actually turned out to be important for the connection between people and also for the therapist's own inspiration. There was a growing understanding that we have to stop judging and wanting to intervene directly. This is what corresponds very closely to the attitude cultivated in the practice of mindfulness, in which we learn to observe and receive everything without judgement.

In addition to these developments in Norway, the Keropudas hospital in Tornio, Finland, decided in 1984 to organise and shape psychiatric care in their whole region in this way. A crisis is seen as a crisis within the social network, and not just as a crisis of the client alone which means that the environment is not capable of coping adequately with the person. According to this vision, admission to a psychiatric hospital is not the result of symptoms, but of the fact that the person in crisis is no longer attuned to others in his environment. Human behaviour always occurs in a context. It was decided to postpone the administration of neuroleptics and admission, previously often used as a quick fix, as much as possible and to focus on other possible support for people in crisis. Psychosis is seen as part of the context, as an attempt to express something that is sometimes difficult for others to understand and that can lead to the isolation of the person concerned (Mackler, 2011). However, other treatments are not excluded and are used on demand as appropriate. The therapeutic team engages in dialogue with the client and his or her network and attempts to promote their mutual understanding so that a common language can emerge. There is often meaning, perhaps something really important behind insights that we do not immediately make sense of.

The introduction to OD and the practice of mindfulness have changed me not only as a psychiatrist but also a lot as a person. I think it has made me more aware and respectful of myself. I work as a psychiatrist in a management role within a large mental health organisation. My excitement about OD has brought me into contact with people who also feel the need to work in this way. It takes a lot of training to become aware of our reflexes and to unlearn them.

There has been some criticism that OD is not new and that research has not yet adequately demonstrated its effect. It has also been said that the situation in Tornio is not very transferable to other countries. Nevertheless, there is little argument against providing good care in this refreshing way. After all, the current approach and neuroleptics for clients with a tendency to psychosis offer moderate results and long-term use of medication is associated with side effects and a shortened life expectancy and there are few suitable alternatives.

Although a full OD model is not possible everywhere, this dialogic approach is spreading, and this can have a beneficial influence not only on the way we work with clients but also on how the professionals work with each other for example at the level of peer supervision, team meetings and management styles. I certainly believe that working and thinking with OD connects us in a healing way with others, but it will take time, patience and equanimity to implement it into the mental healthcare services.

OD and the practice of mindfulness – Kwok Wong

Working with OD involves promoting dialogue and polyphony and tolerating uncertainty. The concepts of 'dialogue' and 'polyphony', which have already been explained above, originate from the ideas of the Russian thinker Mikhail Bakhtin.[1] The seven main principles of OD are as follows:

1. Providing help immediately (within 24 hours)
2. Involving the social network from the very first meeting
3. Flexibility and mobility in terms of duration, place and content
4. Responsibility: the primary practitioner is and remains responsible for the entire process
5. Psychological continuity, by continuing to work with the same team
6. Tolerating uncertainty
7. Promoting dialogue

   Research by, among others, Jaakko Seikkula – who was involved in the development of dialogic network practices in Finland – has shown that the OD approach shows impressive results in the area of recovery after a psychological crisis (Seikkula & Arnkil, 2006).

The emergence of peer-supported OD

Peer-supported Open Dialogue (POD) emerged as a training and care offering in England in 2015, after Russell Razzaque came into contact with OD. He describes this in more detail in the last part of this chapter. He saw similarities between mindfulness and OD, after which he and others set up the POD training course in England. The POD training is based on the following core values openness, authenticity and unconditional warmth. In addition to the general skills associated with the practice of OD, the importance of experiential knowledge, expertise and the practice of mindfulness is explicitly emphasised. OD and mindfulness have several similarities, and I will explore these further below.

The inner attitude at network meetings

Within OD, the network meetings play a vital role. During these meetings, a client/service user enters a dialogue with persons who are important to him or her, together with at least two POD practitioners. Olson, Seikkula and Ziedonis (2014) have described 12 key elements for network meetings:

1. The presence of at least two facilitators
2. Participation in the network
3. Open questions

4. Responding to expressions
5. Emphasising the here-and-now
6. Polyphony
7. Responding to 'problem' expressions or behaviour as meaningful
8. Use of relational sensitivity in the dialogue
9. Expressing the client's own words and stories (rather than symptoms)
10. Reflecting
11. Transparency/openness from the facilitators
12. Finally tolerating uncertainty

I will return to these key elements later in this chapter.

Jon Kabat-Zinn (1990) described seven attitudinal aspects as pillars for the practice of mindfulness: non-judging, patience, beginner's mind, trust, non-striving, acceptance and letting go. In addition, he wrote that mindful attending to thoughts and feelings – especially in relation to others and at times of stress – can help us to deal with pain and stress differently. Shapiro and Carlson (2009) have written about the value and importance of mindfulness in fostering the working alliance in psychotherapy. They describe mindful awareness as a way of being in the body and mind from moment to moment, also as a way of relating to positive, negative and neutral experiences in an open and receptive way.

We can see how mindfulness shows similarities with many of the 12 key elements of the network meetings, both in terms of the attitude of the facilitators, as in how mental health problems are viewed. OD is also explicitly about involving the client's significant others in the process so that they can also make their voices heard and experience their connection with each other. Open questioning requires patience and curiosity in an authentic way. It is also very tempting to focus on symptoms instead of listening to and appreciating someone's own words and stories.

When practising medicine, pattern recognition is important in order to interpret complaints/symptoms. Here, an open mind may seem contradictory, but such an attitude does the most justice to the uniqueness of another person's experiences. Pattern recognition is not necessarily out of the question, but may come up later, and then as one of the possible voices. When we show authentic interest and genuine openness to fresh perspectives, it can really invite and encourage someone to tell their story.

Being present in the here and now

Just as with mindfulness, being present in the here-and-now is emphasised in OD. The facilitator is attentive to feelings, physical sensations and thoughts that arise in response to the words of the other participants in the conversation. Seikkula and Arnkil (2006) write about the importance of people being heard and that this is not just hearing with the ears, but hearing – and responding – with the whole body. The response is not primarily rational, but on a more emotional level in the here-and-now.

It is about polyphony – not only externally, where the voice and opinions of others can be heard, but also internally, where each of the different people present, including the facilitators, can listen to different inner voices. In order to promote polyphony, patience, trust and acceptance are needed, as well as awareness on the part of the facilitators of their own inner polyphony, which may also involve conflicting thoughts. Seikkula and Arnkil (2014) describe the facilitators as embodied human beings, where voices of grief and loss become part of the polyphony when experiencing loss. The inner voices of the facilitator are part of that here-and-now, creating a shared dance of dialogue without the need to express it in words. Many facilitators also experience much more inner and outer resonance in working with OD, and in their work as a facilitator in general, due to this greater embodiment of the principles of mindfulness.

Openness to all experiences

Reflection plays an important role during the network meetings. When Seikkula and his colleagues started with OD, they decided to stop talking about clients and their networks without their presence. They were inspired by Tom Andersen (1991), who once spontaneously had an idea. He was working with a team on a family discussion. A therapist was interviewing the family, and in the next room colleagues were watching from behind a mirror screen. From time to time, the team behind the mirror would consult with the interviewer. At one point, Andersen came up with the idea of doing this out in the open, in front of the family. Andersen and his colleagues immediately saw the added value of sharing in this way. They noticed that there was more equality.

In OD, at least two facilitators are present at a network meeting, so that they can start a conversation and at certain moments ask permission from the network to reflect. In doing so, the focus from the network is temporarily dropped, they turn away from the network somewhat so that the client and his/her network have room to listen and do not have to react immediately. Of course, they do get the opportunity to respond after the reflection. During the reflection, the facilitator can connect to their own polyphony in an open and authentic way in the form of thoughts, feelings, images or metaphors. An open and accepting attitude towards yourself and others is essential for sharing in a tentative and non-judgemental way. Facilitators show that they have heard all those involved and may want to invite them to share more. Different views within a facilitator or between facilitators can also be shared. As a facilitator, reflecting gives you the opportunity to be transparent. However, it is important to express your thoughts carefully. At first, it may seem uncomfortable for clients, loved ones, people involved and teammates to go through a reflection, but we gradually learned that the openness is much appreciated and that the space to listen can lead to the people involved feeling heard and also being more open to themselves and others.

Tolerating uncertainty

An important key element of the network meetings, and one of the main principles of OD, is to tolerate uncertainty. This is easier said than done, especially during an acute crisis in which a client and his or her loved ones experience a great deal of pain and grief. There may also be pressure from other parties to remedy problematic behaviour, for example. As a bystander, you may feel a strong urge or desire to help someone, or at least to be able to do something. People like to explain or clarify things in order to gain more certainty. Tolerating uncertainty requires patience, acceptance, non-striving, letting go and being aware of your own discomfort as a facilitator. As a therapist, in stressful situations, it is tempting to fall back into your role as the so-called expert, but it is also risky. This does not mean, however, that we should not use our expertise. Seikkula and Arnkil (2014) have written about the importance of the professional becoming proficient in dialogues where his or her specific expertise is rooted in the context. They indicate that this seems simple, but it requires the professional to be present in the here-and-now, not only as a professional but also as a human being.

More being than doing

Mindfulness can be described as the transition from a doing mode to a being mode. This form of awareness can help professionals to be present in a different way in a therapeutic relationship, where it's more about being with clients than acting as an expert. We may never really understand the other person, but we can understand their words as well as we can by being present to the thoughts, feelings, images and other sensations that their words (or non-verbal communication) evoke in us.

Besides this presence, it is also about the core values of OD: openness, authenticity and unconditional warmth. Network meetings can be moments of compassionately being together, with attentiveness on the part of the facilitators and the promotion of attentiveness on the part of the client and his/her relatives.

The attitude regarding suffering and recovery

Finally, I would like to discuss the similarities between mindfulness and OD with respect to suffering and recovery. Machteld Huber (2014) has defined health as 'the ability to adapt and self-manage in the face of social, physical, and emotional challenges'. I see recovery primarily as the ability to relate to suffering, and it is the task of healthcare professionals to support the client in this process. Mindfulness is about presence and awareness where suffering is part of life. By not identifying yourself, or identifying less, with the pain/discomfort, you also gain space to be able to relate to it differently. In OD, you involve those close to you in the process, in order to create the necessary space for all those involved to relate to the suffering of themselves and others. Paradoxically the psychological problems may become less or acquire a different meaning if we learn to relate to them differently rather than strive to reduce them.

OD is the most democratic form of care, which, as mentioned, shows similarities with the practice of mindfulness in several areas. OD, however, cannot be practised alone. We can create conditions for ourselves, but ultimately we need a team, and the right organisational conditions too.

My personal story – Heleen Wadman

I was 14 years old and in the third year of secondary school. In that year it became more and more important for me to eat as little as possible. At a certain point, my mother decided to take me to the GP, because I couldn't go on like this. It was not only my weight that worried my mother, but especially the difficulty she had in making real contact with me. The family doctor shared my mother's concerns and referred me to child psychiatry.

I cannot remember how I felt about this therapy. I do remember that I found it interesting to take the assessment tests. I was especially curious about the results. In which way was I different? In what would I score above average? Despite the fact that interesting hypotheses were outlined about an above-average intelligence, highly developed rational thinking skills and a form of fear of failure, there was no real concrete solution. I would get talks, and these were soon supported by medication. Alongside my family life, my life in high school and my life with my friends, I began to develop a new life in child psychiatry: my life as a psychiatric patient.

Instead of gaining more control, I became more and more confused. I went from secondary school to high school and finally stopped going to school in the final exam year because I couldn't cope anymore. My symptoms got progressively worse and the connection with family, friends and school became more and more complicated. My feelings and thoughts became more and more difficult to reconcile with the people around me and were increasingly explained by myself and the people around me on the basis of my psychological suffering. I was sick.

Whereas at first I still had the idea that I had a grip on what was happening, and I had the feeling that I had the choice whether to eat or not, I was now overwhelmed by thoughts, tensions, fears and panic attacks without being able to pinpoint the cause. My inner world became a vortex that held me hostage. At times it would pull me in, locking me inside myself, and at other times all the built-up tension would explode outwards, pushing me beyond all physical, social and societal limits.

An example of this is a period when I was convinced that I was an under-cover agent for the Russian secret service. These images were only visible to me. I walked the streets barefoot, talked about conspiracies and did not want to talk to some people. The images were not actually happening to me in the present but were feelings from the past that were evoked by the situation at that time. I now believe that these images acted as protection. They gave me the feeling that I was part of a greater whole and could therefore withstand the threats in my environment. I clung anxiously to my story as an undercover agent in order not to feel my fear. I was so afraid that I saw any attempt by others to disprove this story as an attack on my existence.

I and others around me learned to see my experiences in the light of the diagnosis. In my longing for stability, I developed a strange kind of fear of (painful) experiences in my inner and outer world and became more and more trapped and claustrophobic inside myself.

I was afraid I would disappear into space, but also of getting stuck in my own oppressive inner world. All my experiences were fuelled by fear – intense, all-encompassing fear, which I was still able to name, but otherwise, it became more and more difficult for me to find words to express what I was experiencing. I was less and less able to share my struggle with those around me. In addition to the struggle within myself, the tension in my contact with those around me also increased. In the absence of my own words, others began to give words to my experiences. People thought up all sorts of hypotheses about what was happening to me. Sometimes I would nod, sometimes I would retort, but in the meantime, I would withdraw further and further. Nobody really understood me.

I realised that I would not be able to endure this life in isolation with all these fears for very long and had thoughts of death. However, I spotted a small pinprick of light behind the fear where life still seemed worthwhile and by chance I found out that this point of light got bigger when I reduced my medication. Looking back, this was the moment I had no choice but to embrace life without fear. At that moment I did not realise what was happening, I just did the only thing I could do to survive, just like all the years before.

In the years that followed all the fearful experiences came up. The difference, however, was that I no longer saw this as a reason to interpret my experiences as a disorder or an episode and thus to put myself down. I increasingly saw it as an opportunity to work with my body and mind to become myself again. This was a lonely struggle and at the same time a connecting search. I noticed that when people did not understand me, they became worried and afraid that I was really ill. Sometimes, I caught myself reacting in the same way. When I succeeded in naming and describing my experience and thus connecting to the experience of the other, trust and connection grew.

It was crucial for my self-confidence to have people who understood me, and to realise that my experiences could be allowed to be. All those experiences that revealed themselves to my senses as little fragments: thoughts, feelings, physical sensations, smells, images and sounds. They were often completely random and did not correspond at all to the situation in the present. It was quite a job to give these experiences of my inner world a place, to let them be and at the same time keep in touch with my surroundings. I experienced a big gap between my intuitive process of healing and the often purely rational approach of my surroundings.

OD and mindfulness as the start of a healing process

Fortunately, I had a few people around me who could act as a sounding board, so that I could create some order again. I desperately needed my surroundings to help me untangle all the tangles. But these people could also sometimes make this process more difficult by making interpretations and judgements that did not fit in with my own world of experiences. We did a fragile dance together, and only during the OD training – which I started in 2017 – I began to understand what I was doing and why.

During the OD training, I came into contact with mindfulness for the first time and things began to make more sense. I understood that as humans we have a constant stream of experiences. We hear, feel, smell, taste, see and think. During meditations, I learned to be aware of these experiences, by noticing them with an open mind. I learned that we essentially have a constant stream of experiences and that we become aware of these experiences when we bring our attention to them. Sometimes we can be reminded of (painful) experiences in the past. Often we then try to push these experiences away by reacting instead of responding. During meditations, I noticed that when you push away experiences, they demand more and more attention, and it becomes increasingly difficult to keep your attention open and consciously shift it.

During a deep meditation, I could see how the mind tends to cling to pleasant experiences (desire) and push away unpleasant experiences (resistance). In the case of unpleasant experiences, we react to our experiences instead of being open to them. We react with physical reactions, such as pain and agitation, or by thinking and creating stories around our experiences. I understood that my treatment had been mostly focused on my experience of thinking, which made my resistance to other experiences grow. I discovered that fear in particular is an emotional experience that we would rather not be aware of. As a reaction, we sometimes create stories about threat and danger so that we do not have to feel this fear.

It was insightful to see that we create these stories ourselves, often neglecting the perceptions of people around us. So when you no longer succeed in sharing your experiences, these stories can sometimes take on a life of their own – think of my story as an undercover agent of the Russian secret service. Before the training, I had always seen this as part of my illness, but now I understand that this was just my way of giving meaning to experiences that I could not place properly and which confused me.

It seemed like nonsense to me at the time, but in fact I was just placing my experiences in the wrong context. The psychiatric treatment was mainly focussing on suppressing my experiences with medication, and their meaning was changed. There was a targeted search for something that I was supposed to be unconsciously trying to suppress. I think you can compare this with looking for a needle in a haystack that doesn't want to be found.

By giving them space, these experiences and stories came closer together again and created a shared experience, a shared meaning. This led to acceptance and safety, in which things could be as they are. From this space, the conditions were created for all those involved to be able to let go of reactions to very painful and disruptive experiences and to get into contact again with what lay below them. And that is what appeared to make it particularly healing; it allowed connections with myself and with the environment to be restored.

The development of OD and a randomised trial in the UK – Russell Razzaque

I had been a psychiatrist for over ten years before I heard about OD or mindfulness. My particular way of working was very much mainstream and all of my thinking was based on assessing symptoms, and then deciding what medication would do the best job at reducing or removing them. I have worked across a number of services over the years, this includes home treatment crisis teams, in-patient services, locked wards – or intensive care units, where people have committed violence and are under a section of the Mental Health Act – and also community recovery teams. In all these settings most of the recovery was perceived to be driven by the medication and there was very little work going on with people at an emotional level.

Meeting the practice of mindfulness

Things started to change for me about 20 years ago; however, when I was sent on my first mindfulness retreat. I turned up on a Friday night, not having had any experience of mindfulness, to a weekend retreat that was going to end on Sunday afternoon. The first thing that I was told was that talking would cease after dinner on Friday and resume again after lunch on Sunday. I was utterly shocked to hear this and bewildered at the idea that I would be in silence all this time. It occurred to me that in the nearly 30 years since I learnt to speak, I had never actually been silent for that long. During the silence, we had multiple meditation sessions guided by the teacher and he made one statement that fundamentally shattered my world and has, I think, turned it upside down ever since.

The statement was simply this: 'Thinking is overrated'.

As a doctor this was heresy to me. I could not believe there was anything in any way wrong with thinking. But while meditating, what I found is that while I continued to think in my head, I also seemed to be feeling differently towards my body. I seemed to be feeling the sensations within it more and feeling increasingly as if I was residing inside my body instead of always in my head. At some point, something shifted in which I felt comfortable with the constant turmoil that was evident in the mind. We all have a constantly active mind but we have other faculties too; a sense of presence that resides in the body, a kind of embodied dimension to our experience. It felt like a new depth and something I think I had touched for the first time that weekend.

When I went back to work on Monday, I felt as if I had been on a six-month vacation. I was so refreshed and totally transformed that I started a regular mindfulness practice thereafter and began going regularly to retreats as a result.

After attending such for a number of years I began to feel a creeping dissonance with my work. On the one hand, I was really learning to sit with all of the emotional pain that exists within our bodies and I was growing to appreciate the value of really being present with it. I was understanding how allowing myself to experience my pain was enabling me to grow. At the same time at work, the only thing I was engaged in was helping people to remove or suppress theirs. Something did not feel right.

I began to search for different treatment modalities and ways of working that might answer some of these questions. I started to look at forms of psychological intervention like Acceptance and Commitment Therapy and mindfulness-based CBT and these grew increasingly appealing to me in my practice. I began to itch for more research and started to engage in some myself. In one of my first studies, I found that better therapeutic relationships between clinicians and patients correlate strongly with better outcomes – studies that others had done before me which I was able then to verify further. Clearly, there was a whole dimension to care that involved how we relate to people – which is based on how we relate to ourselves – that we have been missing, particularly in a medication-dominated way of working.

It was around this time soon after 2010/2011 that I started to hear about OD. I started to read about it, attend workshops and meet some of the pioneers in Finland. It began to occur to me that this is actually what a wholly mindful system actually looks like. Whether the colleagues in Finland realised it or not, what they had done is create a system for being mindfully present with people's distress and thus enable them to do the same, should they choose to.

Of course, OD is not about teaching anyone mindfulness itself but it is actually about the clinicians being able to sit and be present with people's distress and also bring other people engaged in that distress – their family and their network – into the room. It involves us not jumping to conclusions, tolerating uncertainties and instead just being present with the experience – just as we are when we sit to meditate. Of course, there are limitations to this and if the distress is too high and the demand for some kind of escape or medication or other safety measure is needed then clearly that can be provided.

Then in 2013, I got promoted to become Associate Medical Director in my organisation, meaning that I was involved in management and was now part of the senior management team. What I then realised, actually, was that a number of senior managers were also rapidly reaching the conclusion that our current system was not satisfactory. A very large number of referrals were coming through the door and increasing caseloads were building up in our system but very small numbers of people were actually being discharged. This constant rise was not sustainable.

The development of OD in the UK

When realising that I had allies in senior management, I started to tout the idea of training some people in OD. I got approval from executive committees in my own organisation and others and in 2014 we commenced the first OD training in the UK when we trained several teams from across the NHS.

With the help of the Finnish and other pioneers, we were then able to construct a course that could be conducted over one year through four separate residential weeks, which allow people to really immerse themselves in the OD approach and learn from trainers from around the world who would fly in from Finland, America, Norway and other countries. I found that the doctors, nurses, psychologists, social workers and occupational therapists on the course sincerely opened their eyes to the training. Mark Hopfenbeck and I brought mindfulness into the training as a core aspect and we speculated that this would make a big difference to people's ability to work in a dialogical way. I believe that this innovation has proved to be a powerful booster to the dialogical training and every year now, as we train hundreds of people from around the world, it continues to be fundamental to the course. Being able to be present with our own emotions is almost a prerequisite to being able to present with other people's emotions. That is why mindfulness training is so important as it helps us to be present with any impulses we may have to step in and whilst not suppressing them, not acting on them either, just noticing them while we maintain our focus centrally on the person of concern and their family network who we are here to serve. More often than not, we will then notice that the ideas we have are coming from them instead of from us and that makes them so much more powerful as a result.

Another innovation we made in the UK was bringing peer workers into every team and insisting that every training cohort from every team needed at least one peer worker, ideally more, to be a part of it. These numbers have steadily grown as each POD team, as we now call it, has valued their peer workers as core and crucial members of the family they have become.

After this first year of training, we started to build POD teams in several organisations across the country. These were relatively small teams but they were covering significant populations in their area, so I realised this was a good opportunity to do some valuable research. We eventually teamed up with Professor Steve Pilling at UCL, who is perhaps the most senior academic in the mental health sphere in the UK. He is the lead for our NICE (National Institute for Heath and Care Excellence) national treatment guidelines and also the author of a number of studies that form the basis of our current model of care.

The first meeting with Steve feels to me now like a scene from a movie. I started to outline OD to him and before I was halfway through, he started to interject and explain to me that this was the kind of model that he had hoped would have been created when he originally did the research for crisis home treatment teams nearly 20 years ago. we talked about why that had never got off the ground at that time and surmised it might be because we did not train people to work in that way. Working systemically actually requires a significant emotional commitment as well as a theoretical one and that emotional dimension of training – like the mindfulness and other aspects that we give to the staff in POD training, like family of origin and genogram work – is crucial. That is the bit that was missing, as well as an operational structure that facilitated the kind of continuity of care that enabled deeper relationships to bloom.

A randomised trial

He and I then spent a year brainstorming the kind of study that might do these teams justice and potentially have a real impact on the system. We came up with a design of a cluster randomised trial across six sites around the country, recruiting a large number of subjects – over 500 in the end. We then brought together a panel of seven professors from across the UK to make an application to the National Institute of Health Research for a major grant of £2.4 million. It was an audacious ask. We made our submission and held our breath.

A couple of months later we were informed that we were awarded the money and the trial started in 2017. We have now recruited the full quota of subjects that we need for the trial – just under 500 – and this has turned out to be the largest mental health model of care trial in the world at the current time. It has received a great deal of international attention and the dedication of the teams and the staff on the ground has been truly inspiring to see. We have now trained over 600 clinicians from around the world, mainly in the UK, as teams continue to grow and build and strengthen.

The number of people who receive OD in the UK now is therefore growing rapidly. We also have a growing band of advocates – service users and carers who have received this approach to care – who have taken it upon themselves to travel the country to talk about their experience of OD to other managers and people in positions of power in the NHS to try to convince them to start to implement the same. Such is the passion of service users who have experienced OD that they have even written to national newspapers and we have had a couple of large spreads from patients talking about their experience in The Independent and Guardian newspapers.[2]

At this time, of course, the trial is still ongoing, however, we have finished recruitment and we are now in the final two years of follow-up. We will then need to look at the outcomes of the OD group compared to the treatment-as-usual, control group and examine relapse rates, hospitalisation rates and also measures of function. In addition, we will be looking at mechanisms of action, for example, the size and depth of the social network as well as the degree of agency and decision-making autonomy that people have within an OD approach.

A final word

So far this has been a fascinating journey and yet it also feels in many ways like it has only just begun. Our goal is nothing less than to transform the care received by millions of people across the world and, to this end, it feels like a momentum is truly building.

Table 7.1 Resources

RESOURCES
Books and articles: • Jaakko Seikkula & Tom Erik Arnkil (2006). *Dialogical meetings in social networks.* London: Routledge. • Jaakko Seikkula & Tom Erik Arnkil (2014). *Open dialogues and anticipations: respecting otherness in the present moment.* Helsinki: THL. • Russell Razzaque (2015). Mindfulness and Open Dialogue: a common foundation and a common practice. *Context, 138, 45–46.* • Russell Razzaque (2019). *Dialogical psychiatry: a handbook for the teaching and practice of Open Dialogue.* Milton Keynes: Lightning Source Inc.
Documentaries: • Daniel Mackler (Director) (2011). *Open Dialogue: an alternative Finnish approach to healing psychosis.* New York, NY: Truthtraveler Production. See www.youtube.com/watch?v=HDVhZHJagfQ/
Websites: • www.apopendialogue.org – website of the Academy of Peer-supported Open Dialogue (APOD), the professional body for Peer-supported Open Dialogue Training. • www.nyaprs.org/e-news-bulletins/2019/2/1/olson-a-history-of-the-open-dialogue-approach-in-the-us/ – website with explanation by Mary Olson on the history of Open Dialogue in the USA.

Notes

1 See e.g. Tzvetan Todorov (1984). *Mikhail Bakhtin: The dialogical principle.* Manchester: Manchester University Press.
2 See www.theguardian.com/society/2015/mar/12/open-dialogue-approach-mental-healthcare and www.independent.co.uk/life-style/health-and-families/health-news/open-dialogue-the-radical-new-treatment-having-lifechanging-effects-on-people-s-mental-health-a6762391.html.

References

Andersen, T. (1991). *The reflecting team: Dialogues and dialogues about the dialogues.* New York, NY: Norton.

Armstrong, K. (2011). *Twelve steps to a compassionate life.* London: The Bodley Head.

Bartels-Velthuis, A.A., Van den Brink, E., Koster, F., & Hoenders, H.J.R. (2020). The interpersonal mindfulness program for health care professionals: A feasibility study. *Mindfulness, 11,* 2629–2638. https://doi.org/10.1007/s12671-020-01477-5.

Bohlmeijer, E., & Hulsbergen, M. (2013). *A Beginner's guide to mindfulness. Live in the moment.* New York, NY: Open University Press.

Bohlmeijer, E., & Hulsbergen, M. (2018). *Using positive psychology every day. Learning how to flourish.* London: Routledge.

Bohm, D. (1996). *On dialogue.* London: Routledge.

Branley, M. (2009). *Martin let me go.* Summer Palace Press.

Brensilver, M, Hardy, J.A., & Sofer, O.J. (2020). *Teaching mindfulness to empower adolescents.* New York, NY: W. W. Norton & Company.

Chaskalson, M. (2014). *Mindfulness in eight weeks: The revolutionary 8 week plan to clear your mind and calm your life.* London: HarperCollins Publishers.

Chaskalson, M., & Reitz, M. (2018). *Mind time. How ten mindful minutes can enhance your work, health and happiness.* London: HarperCollins Publishers.

Cornell, A.W. (1996). *The power of focusing: A practical guide to emotional self-healing.* Oakland, CA: New Harbinger.

Cox, C.L., Uddin, L.Q., Di Martino, A., Castellanos, F.X., Milham, M.P., & Kelly, C. (2012). The balance between feeling and knowing: Affective and cognitive empathy are reflected in the brain's intrinsic functional dynamics. *Social Cognitive and Affective Neuroscience, 7*(6), 727–737.

Crane, R.S. (2017). *Mindfulness-based cognitive therapy. Distinctive features* (2nd ed.). London: Routledge.

Crane, R.S., Brewer, J., Feldman, C., Kabat-Zinn, J., Santorelli, S., Williams, J.M.G., & Kuyken, W. (2017). What defines mindfulness-based programs? The warp and the weft. *Psychological Medicine, 47,* 990–999.

Crane, R.S., Karunavira, & Griffith, G.M. (editors, 2021). *Essential resources for mindfulness teachers.* London: Routledge.

Donaldson-Feilder, E., Lewis, R., Yarker, J., Whiley, L.A. (December 2021). Interpersonal mindfulness in leadership development: A delphi study. *Journal of Management Education.* doi: 10.1177/10525629211067183.

Downs, J.J., Hopfenbeck, M.S., Lewis, H.M., Parker, I., & Schnackenberg, N. (2022). *The practical handbook of eating difficulties: A comprehensive guide from personal and professional perspectives*. Shoreham by Sea: Pavilion Publishing and Media Ltd.

Ekman, P. (2008). *Emotional awareness: Overcoming the obstacles to psychological balance and compassion. A conversation between the Dalai Lama and Paul Ekman*. New York, NY: Times Books.

Evans, S., & Garner, J. (editors, 2004). *Talking over the years, a handbook of dynamic psychotherapy with older adults*. London: Routledge.

Feldman, C. (2017). *Boundless heart. The Buddha's path of kindness, compassion, joy, and equanimity*. Boulder, CO: Shambhala Publications, Inc.

Feldman, C., & Kuyken, W. (2019). *Mindfulness: Ancient wisdom meets modern psychology*. New York, NY: The Guilford Press.

Fraser, A. (2013). *The healing power of meditation: Leading experts on Buddhism, psychology, and medicine explore the health benefits of contemplative practice*. Boston, MA: Shambhala.

Gendlin, E.T. (1982). *Focusing*. New York, NY: Bantam Books.

Germer, C.K., & Siegel, R.D. (editors, 2014). *Compassion and wisdom in psychotherapy. Deepening mindfulness in clinical practice*. New York, NY: The Guilford Press.

Gilbert, P. (2010a). *The compassionate mind*. London: Little Brown Book Group.

Gilbert, P. (2010b). *Compassion Focused Therapy. Distinctive features*. London: Routledge.

Gilbert, P., & Choden (2015). *Mindful compassion. How the science of compassion can help you understand your emotions, live in the present, and connect deeply with others*. London: Constable & Robinson Ltd.

Gillis Chapman, S. (2012). *The five keys to mindful communication: Using deep listening and mindful speech to strengthen relationships, heal conflicts, and accomplish your goals*. Boston, MA: Shambhala.

Glück, J. (2016). *Weisheit. Die 5 Prinzipien des gelingenden Lebens*. München: Kösel Verlag.

Goleman, D. (1995). *Emotional intelligence: Why it matters more than IQ*. New York, NY: Bantam Books.

Halifax, J. (2019). *Standing at the edge: Finding freedom where fear and courage meet*. New York, NY: St. Martin's Press.

Hanson, R., & Hanson, F. (2018). *Resilient: How to grow an unshakable core of calm, strength, and happiness. 12 tools for transforming everyday experiences into lasting happiness*. London: Rider.

Heriot-Maitland, C., & Longden, E. (2022). *Relating to voices using compassion focused therapy. A self-help companion*. London: Routledge.

Hick, S.F., & Bien, T. (2008). *Mindfulness and the therapeutic relationship*. New York, NY: The Guilford Press.

Huber, M. (2014). *Towards a new, dynamic concept of health: Its operationalisation and use in public health and healthcare, and in evaluating health effects of food* (thesis). Maastricht: Maastricht University.

Kabat-Zinn, J. (1990). *Full catastrophe living: Using the wisdom of your body and mind to face stress, pain and illness*. New York, NY: Delacorte.

Kabat-Zinn, J. (2018). *Meditation is not what you think. Mindfulness and why it is so important*. London: Little, Brown Book Group.

Karpowicz, S., Harazduk, N., & Haramati, A. (2009). Using mind-body medicine for self-awareness and self-care in medical school. *Journal of Holistic Healthcare, 6,* 19–22.

Kashtan, M. (2014). *Spinning threads of radical aliveness: Transcending the legacy of separation in our individual lives.* Auckland, New Zealand: Fearless Heart Publications.

Kirby, J. (2022). *Choose compassion: why it matters and how it works.* St. Lucia, Australia: University of Queensland Press.

Klimecki, O., & Singer, T. (2011). Empathic distress fatigue rather than compassion fatigue? Integrating findings from empathy research in psychology and social neuroscience. In B. Oakley, A. Knafo, G. Madhavan, & D.S. Wilson (Eds.), *Pathological altruism* (pp. 368–383). Oxford University Press.

Koole, W. (2014). *Mindful leadership: Effective tools to help you focus and succeed.* Leiden, the Netherlands: Warden Press.

Koster, F., (2004). *Liberating insight. Introduction to Buddhist psychology and insight meditation.* Thailand: Silkworm Books.

Koster, F., (2007). *Buddhist meditation in stress management.* Thailand: Silkworm Books.

Koster, F., (2014). *The web of Buddhist wisdom: Introduction to the psychology of the Abhidhamma.* Thailand: Silkworm Books.

Kramer, G. (2007). *Insight dialogue: The interpersonal path to freedom.* Boston, MA: Shambhala.

Kramer, G. (2020). *A whole-life path. A lay Buddhist's guide to crafting a Dhamma-infused life.* Seattle, WA: Insight Dialogue Community.

Kramer, G., Meleo-Meyer, F., & Lee Turner, M. (2008). Cultivating mindfulness in relationship: Insight Dialogue and the Interpersonal Mindfulness Program. In S.F. Hick, & T. Bien (red.), *Mindfulness and the therapeutic relationship.* New York, NY: The Guilford Press.

Leu, L. (2015). Nonviolent Communication companion workbook. A practical guide for individual, group, or classroom (2nd ed.). Encinitas, CA: PuddleDancer Press.

Lomas, T., Medina, J.C., Ivtzan, I., Rupprecht, S., Hart, R., & Eiroa-Orosa, F. J. (2017). A systematic review of the impact of mindfulness on the well-being of healthcare professionals. *Journal of Clinical Psychology, 74*(3), 319–355.

Lown, B. (1998). *The lost art of healing: Practicing compassion in medicine.* New York, NY: Ballantine.

Mackler, D. (director) (2011). *Open Dialogue: An alternative Finnish approach to healing psychosis* [documentary]. New York, NY: Truthtraveler Production.

MacLean, P.D. (1990). *The triune brain in evolution: Role in paleocerebral functions.* New York, NY: Springer.

Maex, E. (2014). Mindfulness. In *The maelstrom of life.* Tielt: Lannoo.

Mathew, M.A.F. (1998). The body as instrument. *Journal of the British Association of Psychotherapists, 35,* 17–36.

Meleo-Meyer, F. (2016). Interpersonal practices: A transformational force in the MBIs. In: D. McCown, D.K. Reibel, & M.S. Micozzi, (editors, 2018). *Resources for teaching mindfulness: An international handbook.* Cham: Springer.

Nouwen, H.J.M. (2004). *Out of solitude: Three meditations on the Christian life.* Notre Dame, IN: Ave Maria Press.

Nouwen, H.J.M. (2006). *Bread for the journey: A daybook of wisdom and faith*. New York, NY: HarperCollins.

Olson, M., Seikkula, J., & Ziedonis, D. (2014). *The key elements of dialogic practice in Open Dialogue*. Worcester, MA: University of Massachusetts Medical School.

Parker, I., Coaten, R., & Hopfenbeck, M.S. (2022). *The practical handbook of living well with dementia*. Monmouth, NJ: PCCS Books.

Parker, I., Schnackenberg, J., & Hopfenbeck, M.S. (2021). *The practical handbook of hearing voices: Therapeutic and creative approaches*. Monmouth, NJ: PCCS Books.

Parker, S.C., Nelson, B.W., Epel, E.S., & Siegel, D.J. (2015). The science of presence – A central mediator of the interpersonal benefits of mindfulness. In: K.W. Brown, J.D. Creswell, & R.M. Ryan (Eds.), *Handbook of mindfulness – Theory, research, and practice* (pp. 225–244). New York, NY: The Guilford Press.

Porges, S.W. (2017). *The pocket guide to the polyvagal theory. The transformative power of feeling safe*. New York, NY: W.W. Norton & Company, Inc.

Razzaque, R. (2014). *Breaking down is waking up: Can psychological suffering be a spiritual gateway?* London: Watkins.

Razzaque, R. (2015). Mindfulness and Open Dialogue: A common foundation and a common practice. *Context, 138*, 45–46.

Razzaque, R. (2019). *Dialogical psychiatry: A handbook for the teaching and practice of Open Dialogue*. Milton Keynes: Lightning Source Inc.

Ricard, M. (2015). *Altruism: The power of compassion to change yourself and the world*. London: Atlantic.

Rockwell, I. (2012). *Natural brilliance – A Buddhist system for uncovering your strengths and letting them shine*. Boston, MA: Shambhala.

Rogers, C.R. (1951). *Client-centred therapy*. London: Little, Brown Book Group.

Rogers, C.R. (1977). *On becoming a person. A Therapist's view of psychotherapy*. London: Little, Brown Book Group.

Rosenberg, M.B. (2005). *Practical spirituality. Reflections on the spiritual basis of Nonviolent Communication*. Encinitas, CA: PuddleDancer Press.

Rosenberg, M.B. (2015). *Nonviolent communication: A language of life*. Louisville, CO: Sounds True.

Saunders, P.A., Tractenberg, R.E., Chaterji, R., Amri, H., Harazduk, N., Gordon, J.S. ... Haramati, A. (2007). Promoting self-awareness and reflection through an experiential mind-body skills course for first year medical students. *Medical Teacher, 29*, 778–784.

Schore, A.N. (2012). *The science of the art of psychotherapy*. New York, NY: W. W. Norton & Company.

Segal, S.V., Williams, J.M.G., & Teasdale, J.D. (2013). *Mindfulness-Based Cognitive Therapy for depression: A new approach to preventing relapse* (2nd ed). New York, NY: The Guilford Press.

Seikkula, J., & Arnkil, T.E. (2006). *Dialogical meetings in social networks*. London: Routledge.

Seikkula, J., & Arnkil, T.E. (2014). *Open dialogues and anticipations: Respecting otherness in the present moment*. Helsinki: THL.

Shamay-Tsoory, S.G. (2010). The neural bases for empathy. *The Neuroscientist, November 2010*. https://doi.org/10.1177/1073858410379268.

Shapiro, S.L., Astin, J.A., Bishop, S.R., & Cordova, M. (2005). Mindfulness-Based Stress Reduction for health care professionals: Results from a randomized trial. *International Journal of Stress Management*, *12*, 164–176.

Shapiro, S.L., Brown, K.W., & Biegel, G.M. (2007). Teaching selfcare to care-givers: Effects of Mindfulness-Based Stress Reduction on the mental health of therapists in training. *Training and Education in Professional Psychology*, *1*, 105–115.

Shapiro, S.L., & Carlson, L.E. (2009). *The art and science of mindfulness: Integrating mindfulness into psychology and the helping professions*. Washington, DC: American Psychological Association.

Siegel, D.J. (2007). *The mindful brain: Reflection and attunement in the cultivation of well-being*. New York, NY: Norton.

Siegel, D.J. (2010). *Mindsight. The new science of personal transformation*. New York, NY: Bantam books.

Siegel, D.J. (2020). *The developing mind. How relationships and the brain interact to shape who we are*. New York, NY: The Guilford Press.

Singer, T., & Bolz, M. (editors, 2013). *Compassion. Bridging practice and science* (freely available ebook). Munich: Max Planck Society. See www.compassion-training.org/.

Singer, T., & Klimecki, O.M. (2014). Empathy and compassion. *Current Biology*, *24*, 875–878.

Sofer, O.J. (2018). *Say what you mean: A mindful approach to Nonviolent Communication*. Boulder, CO: Shambhala Publications.

Sternberg, R.J., & Glück, J. (2021). *Wisdom. The psychology of wise thoughts, words, and deeds*. Cambridge: University Press.

Surrey J.L., & Kramer, G. (2013). Relational mindfulness. In C.K. Germer, R.D. Siegel, & P.R. Fulton (Eds.), *Mindfulness and psychotherapy* (pp. 94–111). New York, NY: The Guilford Press.

Taylor, S. (2006). Tend and befriend: Biobehavioral bases of affiliation under stress. *Current Directions in Psychological Science*, *15*(6), 273–277.

Thich Nhat Hanh (2006). *True love: A practice for awakening the heart*. Boston, MA: Shambhala.

Todorov, T. (1984). *Mikhail Bakhtin: The dialogical principle*. Manchester: Manchester University Press.

Trungpa, C. (2007). *Shambhala. The sacred path of the warrior*. Boston, MA: Shambhala.

Van den Brink, E., & Koster, F. (2015). *Mindfulness-Based Compassionate Living. A new training programme to deepen mindfulness with heartfulness*. London: Routledge.

Van den Brink, E., & Koster, F., with Norton, V. (2018). *A practical guide to Mindfulness-Based Compassionate Living. Living with heart*. London: Routledge.

Van der Cingel, M. (2014). Compassion: The missing link in quality of care. *Nurse Education Today*, *34*(9), 1253–1257. doi: 10.1016/j.nedt.2014.04.003.

Wampold, B.E., & Imel, Z.E. (2015). *The great psychotherapy debate: The evidence for what makes psychotherapy work* (2nd ed.). London: Routledge.

West, M.A. (2021). *Compassionate leadership: Sustaining wisdom, humanity and presence in health and social care*. The Swirling Leaf Press.

West, M.A., Baily, S., & Williams, E. (2020). *The courage of compassion: Supporting nurses and midwives to deliver high quality care (freely available ebook)*. London: The King's Fund. See *www.kingsfund.org.uk/publications/courage-compassion-supporting-nurses-midwives*.

Wilson, K.G., & DuFrene, T. (2008). *Mindfulness for two: An acceptance and commitment therapy approach to mindfulness in psychotherapy*. Oakland, CA: New Harbinger.

Wong, Y.J., Owen, J., Gabana, N.T., Brown, J.W., McInnis, S., Toth, P., & Gilman, L. (2016). Does gratitude writing improve the mental health of psychotherapy clients? Evidence from a randomized controlled trial. *Psychotherapy Research, 28*(2), 192–202.

Zimmermann, J., & Coyle, V. (2009). *The way of council*. Wilton Manors, FL: Bramble Books.

Audio Downloads

The following MP3 files can be downloaded from https://www.routledge.com/9781032200521 for personal and non-commercial use.

1. Kindness Meditation – Yourself (Frits Koster)
2. Kindness Meditation – Self and Others (Frits Koster)
3. Broadening the Field (Edel Maex)
4. Wish (Edel Maex)
5. The Five-Minute Method, short version (Rosamund Oliver)
6. The Five-Minute Method, extended version (Rosamund Oliver)

Cooperating Authors

Chantal Bergers has been working as a doctor in General Practice and nursing homes since 1995. Since 2005, she has been training healthcare professionals in the field of palliative care, particularly in the area of finding meaning at the end of life. She has been actively involved in Awareness Centred Deep Listening Training since it first came to the Netherlands and is a registered ACDLT Trainer.

Erik van den Brink studied medicine in Amsterdam, trained to become a psychiatrist/psychotherapist in the UK and worked at innovative mental health clinics in the Netherlands, where he specialised in mindfulness-based and compassion focussed approaches. He teaches at mindfulness training institutes across Europe and co-authored *Mindfulness-Based Compassionate Living* (2015) and *A practical guide to Mindfulness-Based Compassionate* (2018), which describe the MBCL programme he developed with Frits Koster. See www.mbcl.org.

Olaf Galisch was born in 1968 in East Germany. Since 2003, he has worked as a psychiatrist, first in Germany and since 2004 in the mental health sector in the Netherlands. Since 2021, he has been a medical director and psychiatrist in Friesland, where different disciplines work together in outpatient psychiatric care. Olaf has been involved in the development of Peer-supported Open Dialogue (POD) in the Netherlands since 2016.

Sietske de Haan has worked as a mindfulness teacher and coach since 2005. She specialises in training doctors to be more resilient and have more self-compassion and also in training business leaders and others wishing to integrate compassion into their private and professional lives. She has practised vipassana meditation since 1995 and organises and has lead retreats in Holland and Spain since 2014. See www.compassioninbusiness.com/english.

Esther Hasselman is an independent coach, trainer and facilitator who helps people live life fully and consciously, build resilience from the challenges they face and get the most out of their limited time here on the planet Earth. Based in the Netherlands, she has been coaching and training people in mindfulness, compassion, deep listening and mindful communication for the last 12 years. See www.estherhasselman.nl.

Gregory Heffron is the Executive Director of Green Light Communication. In addition to introductory courses, Greg has developed and teaches the Advanced Certification and Teacher Training courses, which have graduates across North America, South America and Europe. He is also a Teacher-Trainer of Mudra Space Awareness – a Tibetan Buddhist mind-body practice. He has been a mindfulness teacher since 2004. He lives in Oakland, California. See www.greenzonetalk.com.

Jetty Heynekamp has worked as a physiotherapist. She has been practising insight meditation since 1982 and has a lot of experience in working with people with physical limitations. She is a certified mindfulness teacher, together with her husband Frits Koster she set up the Trainingsbureau Mildheid & Mindfulness, from which they organise meditation retreats and communication workshops. She is the co-author of several books.

Frits Koster lived as a Buddhist monk in South-East Asia for six years and he has worked since 1994 in the mental healthcare sector. Together with his wife Jetty Heynekamp, he leads meditation retreats. Together with Erik van den Brink, he developed a secular compassion training, which is described in their books *Mindfulness-Based Compassionate Living* (2015) and *A practical guide to MBCL* (2018). See www.compassionateliving. info or www.fritskoster.com.

Edel Maex is a psychiatrist and one of the founders of working with mindfulness. He founded the stress clinic in the Antwerp Network Hospital. He also supervises a zen group in Antwerp. He is the author of several books on mindfulness and Buddhism. See www.levenindemaalstroom.be.

Victoria Norton is a qualified teacher of MBSR and MBCL. She teaches at a community centre and in local government in Bremen, Germany. Originally from the UK, she studied languages, politics and education and worked as a teacher in the school system and adult education before moving into communication management for an international corporation.

Rosamund Oliver qualified as a psychotherapist in private practice in 1996, and then joined the Karuna Institute staff. She founded ACDLT® Deep Listening Training in 2003. This international training supports listeners to develop greater capacity to connect with their innate awareness, insight and compassion while listening both to others and also to themselves. She has studied meditation and compassion methods with many different Buddhist teachers and she is still learning. See www.deeplisteningtraining.com.

Russell Razzaque has been a practising psychiatrist in the UK for over 20 years. He is currently a consultant in a community mental health team in London and has worked as an advisor to the Ministry of Justice, the Home Office and Cambridge University. His areas of interest are Mindfulness and Open Dialogue. He authored several books, including *Dialogical psychiatry: A handbook for the teaching and practice of Open Dialogue* (2019). See www.compassionatementalhealth.co.uk.

Oren Jay Sofer teaches meditation and Nonviolent Communication internationally. He holds a degree in Comparative Religion, is a Certified Trainer of Nonviolent Communication and is a Somatic Experiencing Practitioner for the healing of trauma. He is the author of several books, including *Say what you mean* (2018) and co-author of *Teaching mindfulness to empower adolescents* (2020). Oren is a co-founder of Mindful Healthcare and the founder of Next Step Dharma. See www.orenjaysofer.com.

Chris Trani is an independent coach, consultant and facilitator who helps people build competence and confidence to have conversations they assess as complex, difficult – or even impossible. Drawing on over 30 years of experience, Chris leverages her background as an oncology nurse, a manager, a counsellor, a corporate leadership and communication coach and a mindfulness facilitator to bring a breadth of experience to her clients. See www.whenconversationsmatter.com.

Heleen Wadman experienced psychiatry as a client for many years. She has been using the experience with recovery she gained as a client and her experience with mental healthcare since 2013 as a peer worker and policy officer within the mental healthcare system. She does this to improve both the client's process and the quality of care.

Kwok Hung Wong works and lives in the Netherlands. After finishing the POD-training in England he was fortunate to participate in the first POD-team of the Netherlands in Eindhoven. His interest in mindfulness was further stimulated during the POD-training and also led to be trained as a mindfulness teacher. He is currently one of the trainers of the POD-training in the Netherlands.

Index

Note: text within tables is indicated in **bold** and text within figures is indicated in *italics*.